I0425960

White Mountain National Forest Alternative Transportation Study

June 2011

USDA Forest Service White Mountain National Forest
Appalachian Mountain Club
Plymouth State University Center for Rural Partnerships
U.S. Department of Transportation, John A. Volpe National Transportation Systems Center

REPORT DOCUMENTATION PAGE

Form Approved
OMB No. 0704 0188

The public reporting burden for this collection of information is estimated to average 1 hour per response, including the time for reviewing instructions, searching existing data sources, gathering and maintaining the data needed, and completing and reviewing the collection of information. Send comments regarding this burden estimate or any other aspect of this collection of information, including suggestions for reducing the burden, to Department of Defense, Washington Headquarters Services, Directorate for Information Operations and Reports (0704-0188), 1215 Jefferson Davis Highway, Suite 1204, Arlington, VA 22202-4302. Respondents should be aware that notwithstanding any other provision of law, no person shall be subject to any penalty for failing to comply with a collection of information if it does not display a currently valid OMB control number. **PLEASE DO NOT RETURN YOUR FORM TO THE ABOVE ADDRESS.**

1. REPORT DATE (DD MM YYYY)	2. REPORT TYPE	3. DATES COVERED (From To)
09/22/2011	Study	September 2009 - December 2011

4. TITLE AND SUBTITLE

White Mountain National Forest Alternative Transportation Study

5a. CONTRACT NUMBER

09-IA-11092200-037

5b. GRANT NUMBER

5c. PROGRAM ELEMENT NUMBER

6. AUTHOR(S)

Alex Linthicum, Charlotte Burger, Larry Garland, Benoni Amsden, Jacob Ormes, William Dauer, Ken Kimball, Ben Rasmussen, Thaddeus Guldbrandsen

5d. PROJECT NUMBER

51VXG70000

5e. TASK NUMBER

JMC39

5f. WORK UNIT NUMBER

7. PERFORMING ORGANIZATION NAME(S) AND ADDRESS(ES)

USDA Forest Service White Mountain National Forest, Appalachian Mountain Club, Plymouth State University Center for Rural Partnerships, U.S. Department of Transportation, John A. Volpe National Transportation Systems

8. PERFORMING ORGANIZATION REPORT NUMBER

DOT-VNTSC-USDA-11-01

9. SPONSORING/MONITORING AGENCY NAME(S) AND ADDRESS(ES)

USDA Forest Service White Mountain National Forest
Forest Headquarters
71 White Mountain Drive
Campton, NH 03223

10. SPONSOR/MONITOR'S ACRONYM(S)

USFS WMNF

11. SPONSOR/MONITOR'S REPORT NUMBER(S)

12. DISTRIBUTION/AVAILABILITY STATEMENT

13. SUPPLEMENTARY NOTES

14. ABSTRACT

The White Mountain National Forest (WMNF) is one of the most visited federal lands for recreation in the country, attracting 1.7 million visitors annually. But growth in visitation to the WMNF is increasingly affecting the visitor experience and the WMNF's natural resources. This report documents a planning effort to improve car-free travel options in and around the forest. It documents visitor use trends and transportation issues, explores partnership opportunities for alternative transportation implementation; and identifies options for additional alternative transportation planning or implementation projects. It concludes with recommendations and possible future scenarios for alternative transportation systems.

15. SUBJECT TERMS

alternative transportation system, transit, bicycle, pedestrian, wayfinding, White Mountain National Forest

16. SECURITY CLASSIFICATION OF:			17. LIMITATION OF ABSTRACT	18. NUMBER OF PAGES	19a. NAME OF RESPONSIBLE PERSON
a. REPORT	b. ABSTRACT	c. THIS PAGE			William Dauer
U	U	U	UU		19b. TELEPHONE NUMBER (Include area code) (603) 536-6207

Standard Form 298 (Rev. 8/98)
Prescribed by ANSI Std. Z39.18

Report notes

The USDA Forest Service (USFS) White Mountain National Forest (WMNF), in partnership with the Appalachian Mountain Club (AMC), the Plymouth State University (PSU) Center for Rural Partnerships, and the U.S. Department of Transportation (USDOT) Volpe National Transportation Systems Center (Volpe Center), prepared this study with funds from the Federal Transit Administration (FTA) Paul S. Sarbanes Transit in Parks (TRIP) program. The TRIP program is an annual grant program that distributes roughly $25 million to parks and public lands for planning and implementation of alternative transportation systems. Alternative transportation systems eligible for the TRIP program must provide transportation benefits (as opposed to solely recreational benefits) and must provide alternatives to travel in privately owned vehicles.

The project team included Bill Dauer and Jacob Ormes of the WMNF; Larry Garland and Ken Kimball of AMC; Benoni Amsden and Thaddeus Guldbrandsen of the PSU Center for Rural Partnerships; and Ben Rasmussen, Alex Linthicum, and Charlotte Burger of the Volpe Center Transportation Planning Division. Study tasks were divided among partners as follows:

WMNF

- Purchase additional traffic counters

AMC

- Analyze back country user trends, patterns, and needs
- Coordinate with USFS National Visitor Use Monitoring Survey
- Analyze changes to current WMNF recreation infrastructure that may decrease secondary travel by WMNF users

PSU

- Coordinate research and data collection activities
- Maintain relationships with regional planning commissions, area transportation coordinators, relevant government agencies and providers, non-profit leaders, and business contacts
- Summarize existing front country user information
- Organize and facilitate engagement workshops

Volpe Center

- Collect and analyze traffic counter data
- Organize and facilitate key informant discussions
- Conduct case studies of alternative transportation at comparable public lands
- Organize logistics of Alternative Transportation Stakeholder Workshop
- Develop project alternatives and distribute alternatives to workshop participants
- Coordinate meetings and deliverables of study team
- Summarize workshop results and compile final report

Acknowledgements

The study partners wish to thank the following numerous organizations and individuals who graciously provided their time, knowledge and guidance in the development of this report:

Susan	Arnold	Appalachian Mountain Club
Chris	Thayer	Appalachian Mountain Club
Jim	Jalbert	C&J Bus Company
Ken	Hunter	Concord Coach Lines
Mark	Okrant	Institute for New Hampshire Studies
Howie	Wemyss	Mount Washington Auto Road
Samantha	Kenney Maltais	New Hampshire Branding Initiative
		Northern Community Investment Corporation
Dean	Eastman	New Hampshire Department of Transportation
Larry	Keniston	New Hampshire Department of Transportation Bicycle/Pedestrian program
Jerry	Moore	New Hampshire Department of Transportation Bicycle/Pedestrian program
Ted	Austin	New Hampshire Division of Parks and Recreation
Lori	Harnois	New Hampshire Division of Travel and Tourism Development
Mary	Deppe	North Country Council
Martha	McLeod	North Country Health Consortium
Beverly	Raymond	North Country Transit
Rodney	Ekstrom	Plymouth State University Outdoor Center
Doug	Grant	Plymouth Transport Central
Patsy	Kendall	Plymouth Transport Central
Dave	Govatsky	Retired United States Forest Service / Friends of Pondicherry
Joe	Corrigan	Waterville Valley Cab Company
Mark	Decoteau	Waterville Valley Transit Authority
Jayne	O'Connor	White Mountain Attractions
Michael	Curreri	White Mountain Transit Authority
Ken	Allen	White Mountain National Forest
Stacy	Lemieux	White Mountain National Forest
Susan	Mathieu	White Mountain National Forest

Table of contents

List of figures

List of tables

List of acronyms

Alternative Transportation Systems	ATS
Appalachian Mountain Club	AMC
Annual Daily Traffic	ADT
Bureau of Land Management	BLM
Department of Transportation	DOT
Department of Resources and Economic Development	DRED
Federal Land Management Agency	FLMA
Federal Transit Administration	FTA
Geographic Information Systems	GIS
National Park Service	NPS
Plymouth State University	PSU
Paul S. Sarbanes Transit in Parks	TRIP
United States Forest Service	USFS
National Visitor Use Monitoring	NVUM
Transportation Enhancement	TE

Transportation issues and options:

• Traveler information / wayfinding / signage	TI
• Bicycle and pedestrian	BP
• Transit	TR
• Policy and planning	PP

White Mountain National Forest	WMNF

Executive summary

The scenic beauty and diversity of recreational opportunities at the White Mountain National Forest (WMNF) makes it one of the most popular national forests and one of the most visited federal lands for recreation in the country. Located within a half day's drive of 70 million people, the WMNF attracts 1.7 million visitors annually, while the surrounding area attracts 5-7 million visitors annually. But with popularity increasing among recreational visitors and tourists, growth in visitation to the WMNF has led to increased automobile traffic throughout the region that is increasingly affecting the visitor experience, the WMNF's natural resources, and air quality. Previous studies have identified heavy traffic at peak visitation times that leads to congestion on popular roads, especially the Kancamagus Highway. Unauthorized parking on roadway shoulders creates safety hazards, and is contributing to resource degradation as vehicles park partially in travel lanes or on vegetation.

Previous studies also note that visiting the WMNF without a car is difficult. Though there is limited scheduled bus service to Lincoln and North Conway and charter bus tours bring visitors through the region, travelers arriving at the WMNF by transit would have difficulty traveling around the forest and surrounding towns without private vehicles. An existing patchwork of public and private transit and shuttle services are limited in scope and many operate only seasonally. Yet as fuel prices fluctuate, the Forest Service expects that the number of visitors interested in transit and alternatives to car use will increase.

This report on alternative transportation in the WMNF, funded by the Federal Transit Administration, Paul S. Sarbanes Transit in Parks (TRIP) program, describes the results of a collaborative transportation study undertaken by the United States Department of Agriculture, United States Forest Service (USFS) White Mountain National Forest (WMNF), the Appalachian Mountain Club (AMC), Plymouth State University (PSU) Center for Rural Partnerships, and the U.S. Department of Transportation, John A. Volpe National Transportation Systems Center (Volpe Center). The study goals were as follows:

- Examine visitor use trends and transportation issues;
- Engage stakeholders and explore partnership opportunities for alternative transportation implementation;
- Improve car-free travel options; and
- Identify options for additional alternative transportation planning or implementation projects.

Over the course of the study, the study team researched alternative transportation systems (ATS) at other similar public lands, reviewed transportation existing conditions at WMNF, examined possible non-motorized infrastructure improvements at trailheads and other popular sites in the forest, and recommended locations for additional permanent traffic counters from which more would be learned about visitor use patterns. The study team conducted a series of engagement workshops and key informant discussions. The study team documented the area's transportation issues in four categories, including traveler Information / wayfinding / signage; bicycle and pedestrian; transit; and policy and planning. Using these same four categories, the study team devised transportation options to address those issues. The team then recommended management improvements and bundled options together to create the following alternative transportation scenarios.

Recommended transportation management improvements include the following:

- Strengthen existing / build new relationships;
- Close existing transit service gaps; and
- Conduct additional and ongoing data collection.

Alternative transportation scenarios suggested by the study team are as follows:

- Scenario 1 - Alternative transportation technical advisory committee;
- Scenario 2 - Improved traveler information;
- Scenario 3 - Bicycle and pedestrian infrastructure;
- Scenario 4 - AMC shuttle service expansion;
- Scenario 5 - Shuttle service on the Kancamagus Highway; and
- Scenario 6 - WMNF front country infrastructure improvements.

The following are recommendations for short-term and long-term improvements to ATS in and around the WMNF:

- **Establish and improve relationships among regional transportation stakeholders.** WMNF and its stakeholders can participate in existing transportation committees and planning efforts, such as the North Country Council Transportation Advisory Committee or the New Hampshire Statewide Planning efforts. Eventually, WMNF and its stakeholders may seek to create an alternative transportation technical advisory committee to focus on ATS issues at the WMNF.
- **Enlarge the significance of transportation in updates to the Forest Plan.** The 2005 Forest Plan mentions transportation but provides few goals, objectives, or strategies related to access, mobility, efficiency, resource protection, congestion, parking, bicycling, walking, wayfinding, or traveler information. Addressing these issues in future updates to the Forest Plan may provide policy direction and strategies for improving alternative transportation in the WMNF.
- **Install permanent traffic counters.** The WMNF may install permanent traffic counters to complement those in use by NHDOT and MDOT. Additional counters may be installed in key corridors in the forest, especially outside developed areas, to help the WMNF better understand transportation dynamics in the forest.
- **Seek alternative transportation quick-wins.** Closing existing transit service gaps, expanding a traveler information resource, undertaking low-cost data collection efforts and testing bicycle amenities at one or two key recreation areas and observing resulting usage patterns are all immediate actions WMNF and its stakeholders may undertake to improve alternative transportation.
- **Discuss and consider moving forward with one or more scenarios.** This report presents six scenarios that represent visions for alternative transportation in and around the WMNF. The WMNF and its stakeholders can apply for additional TRIP grants to further study or implement

one or more of these scenarios and can work with nearby towns and the state to leverage transportation enhancement funding with TRIP grant funding.

- **Use the tools created in this study to create additional scenarios.** By documenting transportation issues and options, the study team has provided tools for WMNF and its stakeholders to create new scenarios. By revisiting the issues and related options, follow-on efforts by WMNF and its stakeholders may combine bundles of options to create new scenarios.

1   Introduction

The White Mountain National Forest (WMNF) is located in north-central New Hampshire and southwestern Maine, as shown in Figure 1. The forest comprises the largest publicly-owned block of land in the six New England states. One of the first national forests established by the Weeks Act in the early 20th century, the WMNF is a national landmark known for responsible resource extraction, natural resource protection, and recreation and tourism, encompassing approximately 800,000 acres of spruce and northern hardwoods. The WMNF includes 1,200 miles of hiking trails, 160 miles of the Appalachian National Scenic Trail, 400 miles of snowmobile trails, 175 trailheads or day use areas, and 23 developed campgrounds. Approximately 157 miles of road provide access to the WMNF, 100 miles of which comprises the White Mountain Trail, a designated byway. Of the 175 trailheads and day use areas, 100 sites are located along the White Mountain Trail.

Figure 1 - WMNF regional location.

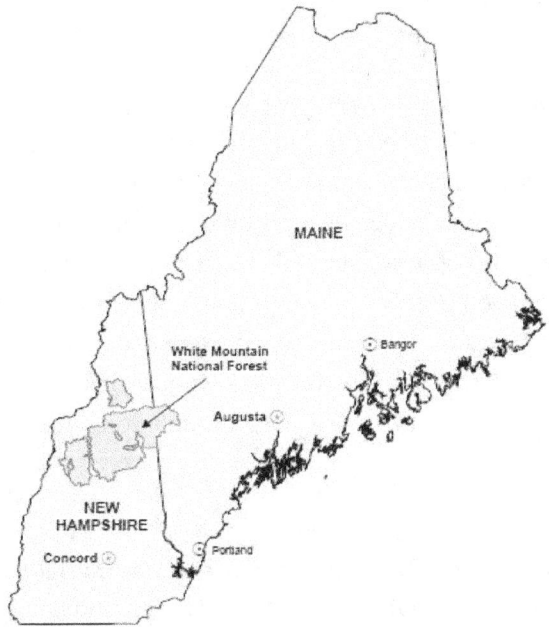

The diversity of recreational opportunities at the WMNF makes it one of the most popular national forests and one of the most visited federal lands for recreation in the country. Located within a half day's drive of 70 million people, the WMNF attracts 1.7 million visitors annually, while the surrounding area attracts 5-7 million visitors annually. Though the WMNF experiences peak visitation periods in the summer months and the fall foliage season, the forest provides year-round recreational resources including hiking, camping, mountain biking, wildlife watching, fishing, hunting, picnicking, swimming, canoeing/kayaking, foliage viewing, snowshoeing, snowmobiling, alpine and nordic skiing, ice climbing, and driving for pleasure. A number of major activity centers are also located on or immediately adjacent to the WMNF, including eight Nordic and alpine ski areas, Appalachian Mountain Club (AMC) huts and hiker facilities, state parks, and a major outlet center in North Conway, NH. The WMNF is one of the focal points of the regional tourism industry, a significant component of New Hampshire's economy.

With popularity increasing among recreationists and tourists, growth in visitation to the WMNF has led to increased automobile traffic throughout the region that is increasingly affecting the visitor experience, available parking, the WMNF's natural resources, and air quality. Heavy traffic at peak visitation times often leads to congestion on popular roads throughout the White Mountains region, especially the Kancamagus Highway. Unauthorized parking on roadway shoulders creates safety hazards and is contributing to resource degradation as vehicles may park partially in travel lanes, or on vegetation.

Despite the challenges caused by personally owned vehicles, visiting the WMNF without a car is difficult. Limited scheduled bus service to Lincoln and North Conway exists, and charter bus tours periodically bring visitors, but a traveler arriving at the WMNF by transit would have difficulty travelling around the forest without a car. An existing patchwork of public and private transit and shuttle services are limited in scope and many operate only seasonally. Yet as fuel prices fluctuate, the Forest Service expects that the number of visitors interested in transit and alternatives to car use will increase.

This report, funded by the Federal Transit Administration, Paul S. Sarbanes Transit in Parks (TRIP) program, describes the results of a transportation study of the WMNF. The TRIP program is an annual grant program that distributes roughly $25 million to parks and public lands for planning and implementation of alternative transportation systems (ATS). Alternative transportation systems eligible for the TRIP program must provide transportation benefits (as opposed to solely recreational benefits) and must provide alternatives to travel in privately-owned vehicles. Four organizations collaborated on this effort, including the United States Department of Agriculture, United States Forest Service (USFS) White Mountain National Forest (WMNF), the Appalachian Mountain Club (AMC), Plymouth State University (PSU) Center for Rural Partnerships, and the U.S. Department of Transportation, John A. Volpe National Transportation Systems Center (Volpe Center).

2 Study information, describes the study in greater detail by defining the study area, summarizing previous study efforts, and stating the study goals and objectives. *3 Alternative transportation systems* describes ATS in general and presents lessons learned from other public lands. *4 Existing conditions* presents transportation existing conditions in the WMNF and describes types of user groups and their travel needs and behaviors; summarizes results from several surveys regarding the transportation preferences of WMNF visitors; summarizes results of outreach activities related to transportation preferences; analyzes traffic counter data and recommends locations for additional permanent counters; inventories area transit systems and transit gaps; inventories existing and planned bicycle infrastructure; reviews pre-trip traveler information resources; and analyzes WMNF infrastructure to identify potential transit nodes and to reduce traffic and parking congestion. *5 Alternative transportation issues and options* presents a summary of the transportation issues and options as identified by the study team and verified by area stakeholders. *6 Transportation scenarios* recommends transportation management improvements and presents six alternative transportation scenarios comprised of sets of transportation options described in the preceding chapter. *7 Next steps /*

recommendations presents next steps and recommendations for alternative transportation in and around the WMNF.

2 Study information

2.1 Study area

The study team defined the study area as the boundaries of the WMNF and surrounding roads, though it also considered opportunities to improve connections among the forest and gateway communities including Lincoln, Conway, North Conway, Gorham, Berlin, Twin Mountain, and Franconia. Figure 2 illustrates the WMNF study area, US Forest Service locations, and gateway communities.

Figure 2 - WMNF study area. Source: AMC

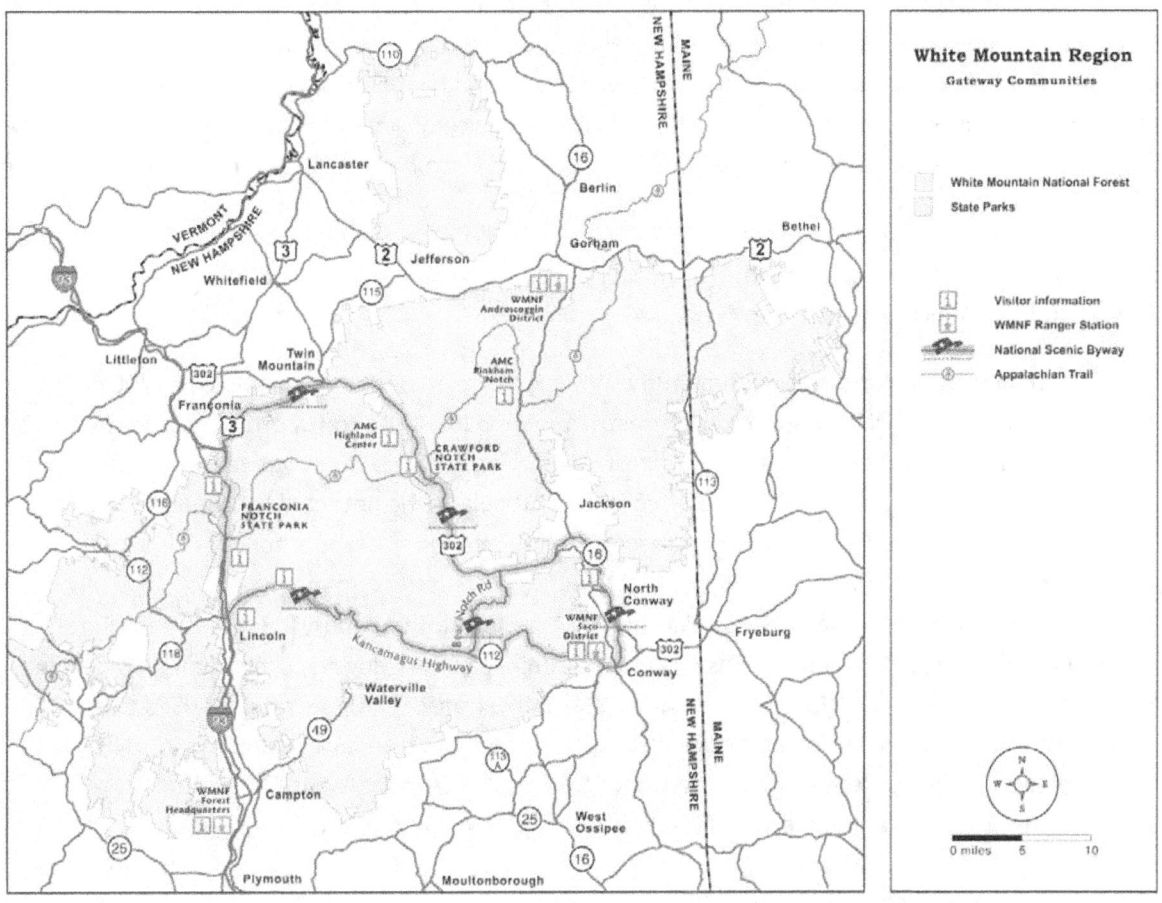

Access to the WMNF is primarily via Interstate 93 and state highways that encircle and pass through the region. The Kancamagus Highway (NH Route 112), Route 16 through Conway and North Conway, NH, and US Route 302, major transportation corridors for NH, are part of a 100-mile National Scenic Byway that transects the WMNF commonly known as the White Mountain Trail. Forest Service roads connect within this network and provide access to many recreational and cultural opportunities.

Although not within WMNF, a number of major activity centers are adjacent, generating their own visitation and sharing visitors with the WMNF. Franconia Notch State Park, located along I-93, includes a number of popular tourist attractions, like the Cannon Mountain Aerial Tramway, the Flume Gorge, and the (former) Old Man of the Mountain Viewing Area. Crawford Notch State Park, is on U.S. 302, and has popular hiking and camping areas, and the AMC Highland Center at Crawford Notch, includes a hiker lodge and outdoor education center. The towns of Conway and North Conway are popular vacation areas with golf courses, outlet shopping malls, and numerous commercial tourist attractions. Additional commercial tourist attractions are on U.S. 3 in the vicinity of Lincoln and U.S. 2 in the vicinity of Gorham.

2.2   Previous transportation planning

The study team built its efforts upon those of the following several previous studies and recent regional transportation planning efforts:

- **Transportation Assistance Group Study** (WMNF, Volpe Center, and stakeholders, 2007). Investigates WMNF transportation infrastructure and Identifies transportation issues facing the WMNF region including, roadway congestion, parking facilities at or over capacity, natural resource degradation, and road user conflicts particularly the potential for conflicts among motor vehicles and bicycles. For more information, see the full report here: http://www.volpe.dot.gov/publiclands/projects/docs/whitemountain.pdf
- **White Mountain National Forest Alternative Transportation Report** (PSU Center for Rural Partnerships, 2009). Summarizes research, planning, and existing transportation providers in and around the WMNF region, describes alternative transportation strategies used to enhance the visitor experience in parks, forests, and other recreation areas, and surveys WMNF visitors, regarding their potential use of alternative transportation in the WMNF region.
  For more information, see the full report here: http://www.plymouth.edu/center-for-rural-partnerships/120/wmnf/
- **Federal Lands Alternative Transportation Systems Study** (Cambridge Systematics, 2003). Highlights the WMNF region and the potential threats to forest resources, air quality, and parking availability that may occur due to an increase in visitation and automobile traffic and includes several suggestions for a bus shuttle route through the WMNF.
  For more information, see the full report here:
  http://www.fta.dot.gov/documents/Fed_Lands_Forest_Service_SupplementATS_Needs.pdf
- **North Country Council Regional Transportation Plan** (North Country Council, 2009). Considers the existing conditions of public transit and human service transportation in the region with the goal of increasing mobility, specifically by filling gaps in existing transportation systems, including recommendations and action items to coordinate regional transportation planning

efforts. For more information, see the full report here:
http://www.nccouncil.org/publications.php

Combined findings from these studies identify the following transportation problems and opportunities:

- Parking overflows near trailheads, scenic vistas, and swimming areas;
- Parking on roadway shoulders causes potential safety hazards and resource damage;
- Congestion occurs on area roads, particularly the Kancamagus Highway;
- Potentials exist for user conflicts on roads, especially between motor vehicles and bicycles;
- Parking expansion would result in unacceptable impacts on adjacent rivers and wetlands;
- Transit service would allow visitors to enjoy the scenery;
- Potential opportunities exist to provide interpretive services on transit vehicles; and
- Opportunities exist for collaboration among regional stakeholders.

Figure 3 illustrates roadway shoulder parking overflow along the Kancamagus Highway.

Figure 3 - Kancamagus Highway, shoulder parking. Source: AMC

Additionally, survey results from PSU's 2009 WMNF Alternative Transportation Report (described above) help to illustrate the perceptions and attitudes of residents in the communities surrounding the WMNF regarding alternative transportation issues. The survey administered to visitors along the Kancamagus Highway (between Lincoln and Conway) reveals that many visitors tend to be local to the WMNF, their visits are for a short period of time (two days or less), and they primarily visit to sightsee and hike.

The survey's alternative transportation findings revealed the following:

- 9.6% of respondents considered alternative transportation to travel from their home to WMNF;
- 19.7% of respondents considered alternative transportation for travel in and around the WMNF;
- No clear relationships between visitor activity and interest in alternative transportation were found;
- Convenience and availability were the two primary deterrents to the use of alternative transportation.

Findings from the efforts listed above suggest both opportunities and obstacles for the development of alternative transportation in the WMNF region. These findings helped to shape the goals identified in the next section.

2.3 Goals and objectives

The study team developed the goals of this study to be aligned with the goals of the TRIP program (the funding source for this study and described in the Introduction), and the 2005 WMNF Forest Plan (2005). The goals of this study are to:

- Examine visitor use trends and transportation issues.
- Engage stakeholders and explore partnership opportunities for alternative transportation implementation.
- Improve car-free travel options.
- Identify options for additional alternative transportation planning, or implementation projects.

Goals of the TRIP program include:

- Conserve natural, historical, and cultural resources
- Reduce congestion and pollution
- Improve visitor mobility and accessibility
- Ensure access to all, including persons with disabilities

The relationships between this study's goals and the TRIP program goals are shown in Figure 4.

Figure 4 - Relationships between study goals and TRIP program goals.

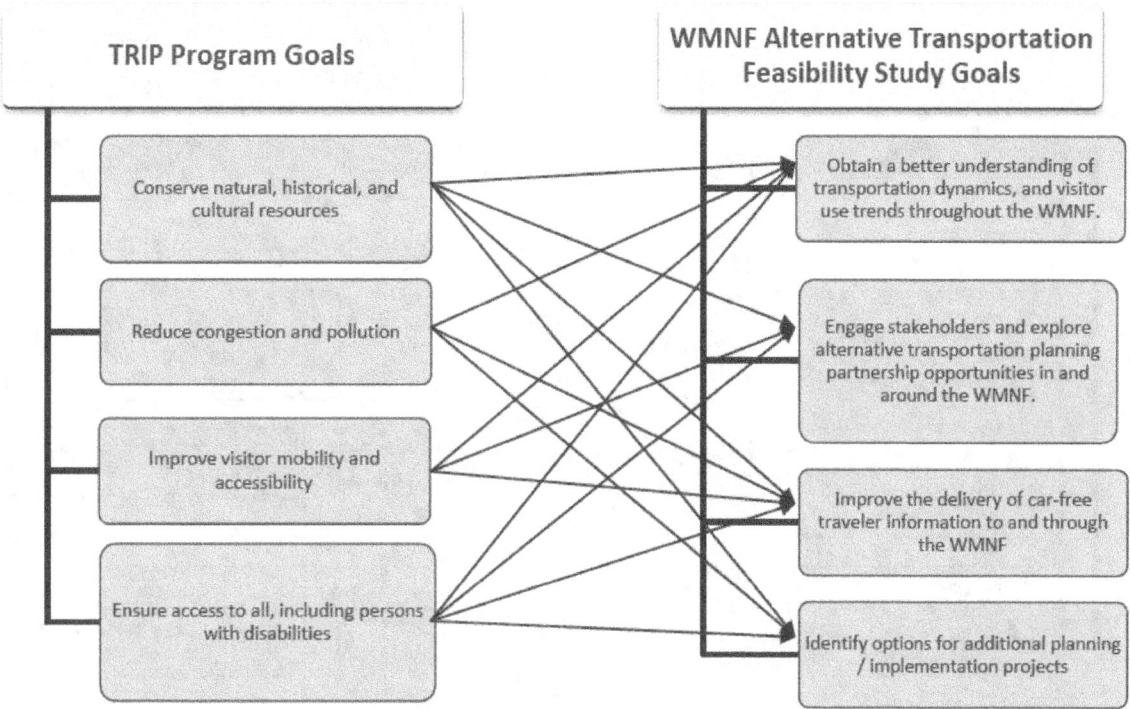

The Forest Plan is the long-range planning document that guides Forest Service plans for resource management and protection, and provides direction for all management programs, practices, uses of forestlands, and protection and conservation measures. The Forest Plan does not provide many details regarding transportation or alternative transportation, though it does include the following transportation-specific:

- Provide a safe, efficient, and seamless transportation and parking network that allows for current, continued, and projected management, use.
- Look for and analyze alternative transportation opportunities to deal with projected increases in traffic and parking volumes.
- Work cooperatively with state, county, and town officials.
- Maintain and update the US Forest road inventory and index as management decisions are made, and through monitoring and field verification.

The relationships between this study's goals and the Forest Plan transportation-specific goals are shown in Figure 5.

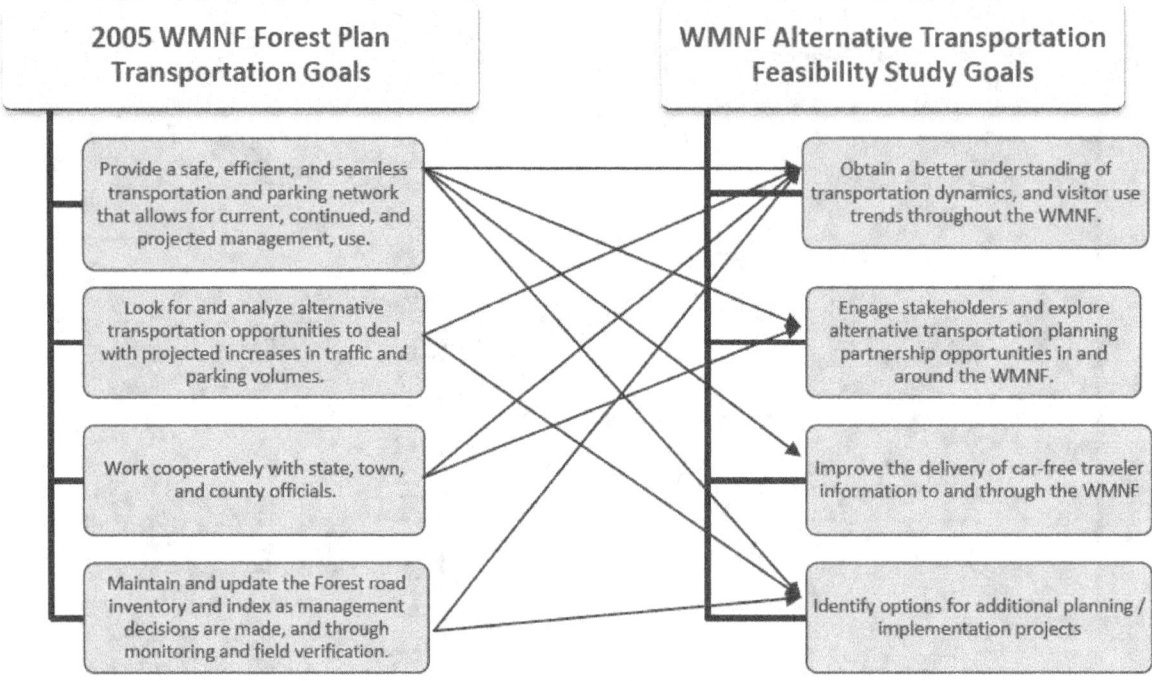

The WMNF Forest Plan includes some goals that are not specific to transportation but are aligned with goals of ATS. These non-transportation Forest Plan goals include:

- Reduce adverse effects of air pollution on forest ecosystems.
- Maintain or improve public access to US Forest Service lands.
- Work with partners and volunteers to sustain natural and cultural resources.
- Provide a variety of recreation opportunities for people with disabilities and continue to improve accessibility to recreation sites.

The relationships between this study's goals and the Forest Plan non-transportation goals are shown in Figure 6.

Figure 6 - Relationships between study goals and the Forest Plan non-transportation goals.

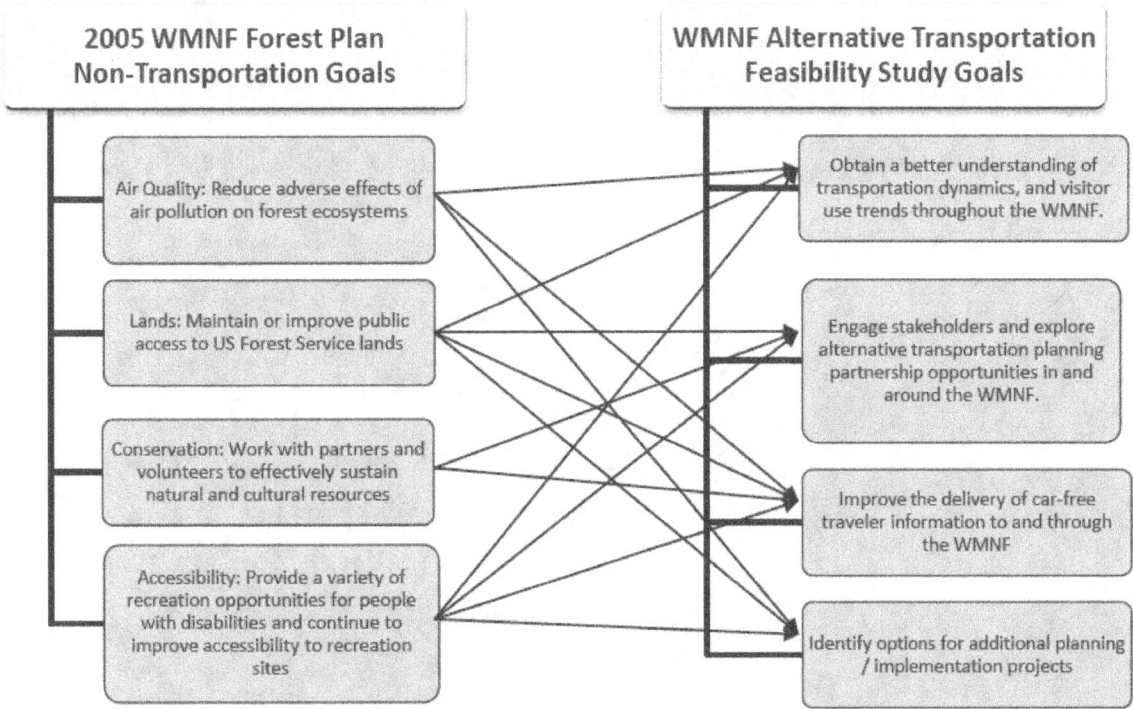

More information about the goals and types of ATS is provided in the following chapter.

3 Alternative transportation systems

Alternative transportation systems (ATS) are those transportation systems which provide alternatives to use of privately owned vehicles in an effort to reduce traffic and parking congestion, reduce natural resource conflicts, reduce greenhouse gas emissions, and improve comfort and convenience for travelers. Federal land management agencies (FLMAs) throughout the country have implemented ATS to achieve these goals.

The TRIP program defines ATS as "transportation by bus, rail, or any other publicly available means of transportation and includes sightseeing service. It also includes non-motorized transportation systems such as pedestrian and bicycle trails."[1] In addition, traveler information systems, including wayfinding signage, traveler information websites, or transportation safety studies, are eligible funding activities under the TRIP program because these elements may improve, resource management, visitor experience and mobility, and automobile congestion and air, noise, and visual pollution.[2] Table 1 describes four categories of ATS considered by the study team.

Table 1 - Alternative transportation system types and descriptions.

ATS Type	ATS Description
Traveler information / wayfinding / signage	Interactive and/or static web-based traveler information and roadside/trail signage that may be delivered pre-trip, en route, or post-trip.
Bicycle and pedestrian	Non-motorized connections among communities and recreation opportunities that create a means of travel for cyclists and pedestrians.
Transit	Small, medium, and large scale bus, shuttle or van systems that provides a publically available alternative to the use of a private vehicle.
Policy and planning	Decisions regarding infrastructure investments, partnerships, and operations and management that help to shape and support the environment for effective ATS planning and implementation.

Figure 7 through Figure 10 illustrate example components of ATS.

---

[1] Alternative Transportation in Parks and Public Lands, Program Manual. January 2007. U.S. Department of Transportation, Federal Transit Administration. FTA-MA-20-1001-06.1 Accessed January 25, 2011. P. 13 <http://www.fta.dot.gov/documents/ATPPL_Manual_1-9-07.pdf>
[2] *Ibid.*

Figure 7 - Bicycle wayfinding signage.
Source: City of Gresham, Oregon

Figure 8 - Franconia Notch Bicycle path.
Source: NH Division of Forest and Lands

Figure 9 - Schulykill River National and State Heritage Area online trip itinerary planner.
Source: Schulykill River Greenway Association

Figure 10 - Bureau of Land Management/Lassen Rural Bus shuttle.
Source: Bureau of Land Management

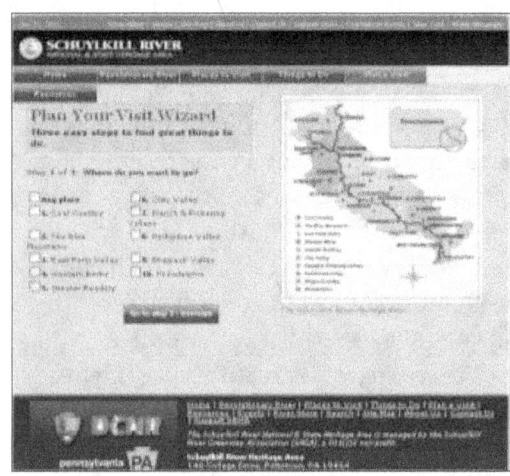

3.1 ATS peer comparison

In order to identify ATS solutions, lessons learned, and best practices that might be applicable to the WMNF, the study team compiled case studies of ATS on other similar public lands units. Units were chosen based on similarities in geography, annual visitation, recreational opportunities, etc. The case studies themselves are provided in *Appendix A – Alternative transportation system peer comparison*, and short summaries are below:

- **Bureau of Land Management Eagle Lake Field Office** has dispersed visitation spread among a variety of destinations, similar to the numerous trailheads within the WMNF. The past partnership between the Bureau of Land Management and the local transit provider to provide transit to the Bizz Johnson trial offers lessons learned for supplying an alternative to private vehicle access to a specific trailhead destination.

- **North Moab Recreation Areas**, including Arches National Park and the Bureau of Land Management Moab Field Office, consists largely of dispersed trailheads. To create opportunities for alternative transportation in the area, a transportation hub is being planned that will centralize travel destinations to a single location, and facilitate trail access by means other than private automobiles.
- **Delaware Water Gap National Recreation Area** has several main roads that experience a great deal of commuter and cut-through traffic, much like the roads in WMNF. One road and several bridges utilize tolls to mitigate traffic and fund maintenance and operations of the unit's transportation infrastructure.
- **White River National Forest**, like WMNF, is a national forest that experiences extreme seasonal peaks in visitation. The Maroon Bells Shuttle service provides an instructive case of how this land unit partners with the local Roaring Fork Transit Authority to manage visitor demand on a single scenic road during peak season.
- **Sequoia National Park** is only several hours' drive from major urban population centers in San Francisco and Los Angeles. WMNF is a similar distance from Boston. A cooperative agreement between the National Park Service and the city of Visalia to provide shuttle service to and throughout the park provides a model for reducing automobile congestion and greenhouse gas emissions.
- **Zion National Park** and its transit system are tightly integrated with the gateway community, Springdale, much the same way that WMNF has the potential to create symbiotic transportation relationships with Lincoln, Conway, or other gateway communities.
- **Acadia National Park** experiences annual visitation of approximately 2 million people. Though it is a fraction of the size of WMNF, and its island geography creates natural constraints on the travel network that favors transit, the Island Explorer bus system provides a case study for innovative partnerships in the delivery of transit service.

Several success factors are common to the ATS's listed above:

- **Partnering with local transit providers allows FLMAs to focus on the land rather than on operations and maintenance of a transit system**. Most federal land units are not equipped to staff, maintain, and operate a transit system. Transit systems must meet an array of federal requirements in terms of accessibility and system design. Vehicle drivers and mechanics with specific skill sets, and maintenance, fueling, and storage facilities on or near the public lands are also necessary. Partnering with local transit service providers allows agencies with transit operations and maintenance experience and resources to assume the responsibility for system operations. Partnerships with local chambers of commerce, retailers, etc. may provide a means, often at little cost to the federal land unit, to support the system, for example through partnership marketing, advertisement, or other methods of cross promotion.
- **Implementing policy constraints on private vehicle access can help support resource management goals and transit systems.** Successful transit systems on federal lands are often accompanied by policies that constrain automobile parking and/or private vehicle access or are located in areas with limited or expensive parking. The shuttle systems at Zion National Park and

at White River National Forest are mandatory for visitors during peak visitation season, necessitating the use of the shuttle to experience the park. The shuttle system at Acadia is not mandatory, although parking in the surrounding town of Bar Harbor is limited to a two-hour period, which may provide an incentive to use the bus system if visitors intend to stay longer. This season, Sequoia staff tested closing a portion of the main road through the park to vehicle traffic during select historically high-visitation weekends. Severe traffic congestion was eliminated, and shuttle ridership increased significantly during those days.[3]

- **Marketing and advertising a transit system service is essential.** Information that is publicly accessible, easily understood, and provided through several distribution channels (internet, print, television, radio, smart phone, etc.) is key to communicating the availability and functions of a transit service. If a transit system is not mandatory, making buses or shuttles an attractive alternative to private automobiles is an ambitious goal. In these cases, marketing that targets potential riders' personal connection to the outcomes of using transit may influence their decisions to use the system. For example, motivating factors for transit use may include the desire to reduce transportation costs, time spent traveling, stress associated with driving/searching for parking, and contributing to pollution. Often transit use may be chosen for the unique experience it offers when on-board interpretive services is featured, or access to non-public roads and areas is provided.

- **Ensuring a continued source of operations and maintenance funding is often overlooked**. Few transit systems are funded entirely on farebox revenues. The TRIP Program that funded many of the transit systems mentioned in this comparison does not fund transit system maintenance and operating costs. Public funding mechanisms may not increase at the same rate as inflation, and funding from public sources may fluctuate from year to year. Partnerships, use of recreation enhancement fees, or use of a federal lands unit operating funds may also subsidize operations costs.

In addition to the success factors listed above, Table 2 summarizes lesson learned from the case studies as well as how the lessons may relate to the WMNF.

---

[3] Personal communication with City of Visalia transportation department staff.

Table 2 - Summary of ATS peer comparison key lessons and opportunities.

Public land unit	Lessons	Opportunities
Bureau of Land Management Eagle Lake Field Office	• Provides an example of transit service with a bicycle hauling feature to popular trail locations. • Public transit agencies must adhere to Federal Transit Administration regulations regarding community-based charter services, namely, such services may only be provided in cases for which a service would not otherwise be cost-effective manner for private operators.[4]	• WMNF and nearby areas have several popular bicycle loops that may be appropriate for a similar service.
North Moab Recreation Areas, including Arches National Park and the Bureau of Land Management Moab Field Office	• Illustrates a multi-faceted alternative transportation project, including a transportation hub, a pedestrian/bicycle bridge, and trails that create a junction for several modes of travel (e.g. automobile, transit, bicycles, and pedestrians) and access to the Town of Moab, and other popular recreation areas. • Funded by a variety of partners and, in large part, by the TRIP program.	• WMNF may consider the construction of a similar facility, scaled appropriately, to improve visitor contact with the USFS, and to act as a place to provide traveler information, and to consolidate travel and recreational activities like hiking and biking between/among various locations throughout the area.
Delaware Water Gap National Recreation Area	• DEWA tolls commercial vehicles on Rt. 209 • DEWA's website promotes public transportation to the park.	• DEWA's toll system provides a potential model to WMNF regarding the Kancamagus Highway or other roads. Though DEWA authority to toll is mandated by the legislature, WMNF could investigate the option as a means to limit access to privately-owned vehicles. • WMNF use its website to communicate public transportation options to access forest sites.
White River National Forest	• Operates a mandatory shuttle system on main scenic roadway, funded in part by FLREA fees.	• WMNF may consider a similar service on the Kancamagus Highway, or other roads with heavy visitor traffic and access needs.

---

[4] Federal Transit Administration. http://www.fta.dot.gov/printer_friendly/leg_reg_180.html

Public land unit	Lessons	Opportunities
Sequoia National Park	• Demonstrates a strong partnership between the park and the gateway community of the City of Visalia. System includes a shuttle route between Visalia and the park and two in-park shuttle routes. The entire system is operated by local City of Visalia, funded in part by TRIP, CMAQ, and economic development grants.	• WMNF may consider partnerships with Conway, Lincoln, Woodstock or other areas as gateway communities to the forest.
Zion National Park	• Demonstrates a strong partnership between the park and the gateway community of Springdale, including the provision of a centralized parking area and shuttle pick-up location to stage visitation to Zion. Provides realistic operations and maintenance costs for a large scale transit system.	• WMNF may consider partnerships with Conway, Lincoln, Woodstock or other areas as gateway communities to the forest.
Acadia National Park	• Provides a case study for innovative public-private partnerships, where the transit system is operated and maintained through an extensive partnership of federal, state, and local government funds and contributions from small local businesses, and a major multi-year grant from the well-known L.L. Bean clothing manufacturer.	• WMNF may consider a similar business model that draws upon public funding and private support from local resorts, or other businesses that would benefit from improved visitor circulation through the forest from commercial destinations.

The lessons and opportunities learned from ATS systems at other federal land units were used to develop some of the transportation options described in *5.2 Alternative transportation options* and scenarios described in *6 Transportation scenarios*.

4   Existing conditions

This section describes the existing transportation conditions in the White Mountains region. It addresses the study goal of examining visitor use trends and transportation issues in and around the WMNF. Specifically, this section describes types of user groups and their travel needs and behaviors; summarizes results from several surveys regarding the transportation preferences of WMNF visitors; summarizes results of outreach activities related to transportation preferences; analyzes traffic counter data and recommends locations for additional permanent counters; inventories area transit systems and transit gaps; inventories existing and planned bicycle infrastructure; reviews pre-trip traveler information resources; and analyzes WMNF infrastructure to identify potential transit nodes and to reduce traffic and parking congestion.

4.1   Visitor group types

The natural beauty, interesting topography, and recreational infrastructure within the White Mountains region attract visitors with diverse recreational interests to the area. Although there are many ways to categorize transportation users in and around the WMNF (e.g., by activity type, by mode, by age, etc.) the study team considered four types of visitor groups by intensity of use. Doing so allowed the study team to identify varying levels of alternative transportation needs. These visitor group types are described below and in Figure 11.

- **Backcountry visitors** desire access to back-country trailheads often for multiple-day trips. This group travels with gear, including hiking packs, sleeping bags, cooking implements, and water purifying equipment. They may be open to using public or private shuttles in order to avoid driving, parking, and ensuring secure storage of a vehicle while on extended multi-day trips.

- **Front-country visitors** desire access to front-country trailheads and day-use area, and generally visit an area for several hours. This group often visits multiple sites within a day / trip and combines visits to the WMNF with other nearby activities (sight-seeing, shopping, dining, etc.). This group may include families with small children. This group may travel with some gear, and values convenience and accessible access to picnic locations, and natural features for day-long excursions. If available, convenient, and or safe this group may use alternative transportation as a means to travel to sites within the WMNF.

- **Tourists and sightseers** require access to popular day use areas generally by private vehicle. This group often visits multiple sites within a day / trip and combines visits to the WMNF with other nearby activities (sight-seeing, shopping, dining, etc.). This group may include families with small children. This group travels with little gear, and generally value comfort and convenience. This group may not be familiar with the area; therefore, the use of alternative transportation requires incentives, clear marketing, and ease of use.

- **Through-travelers** require access on major roads through the WMNF, and value convenience and low traffic volumes. The Forest Service has little influence over the travel behavior of these users.

The study team primarily considered the use characteristics and needs of back-country visitors, front-country visitors, and tourists and sightseers. Improving alternative transportation for through-travelers was not a focus of this study.

Figure 11 - WMNF user group categories.

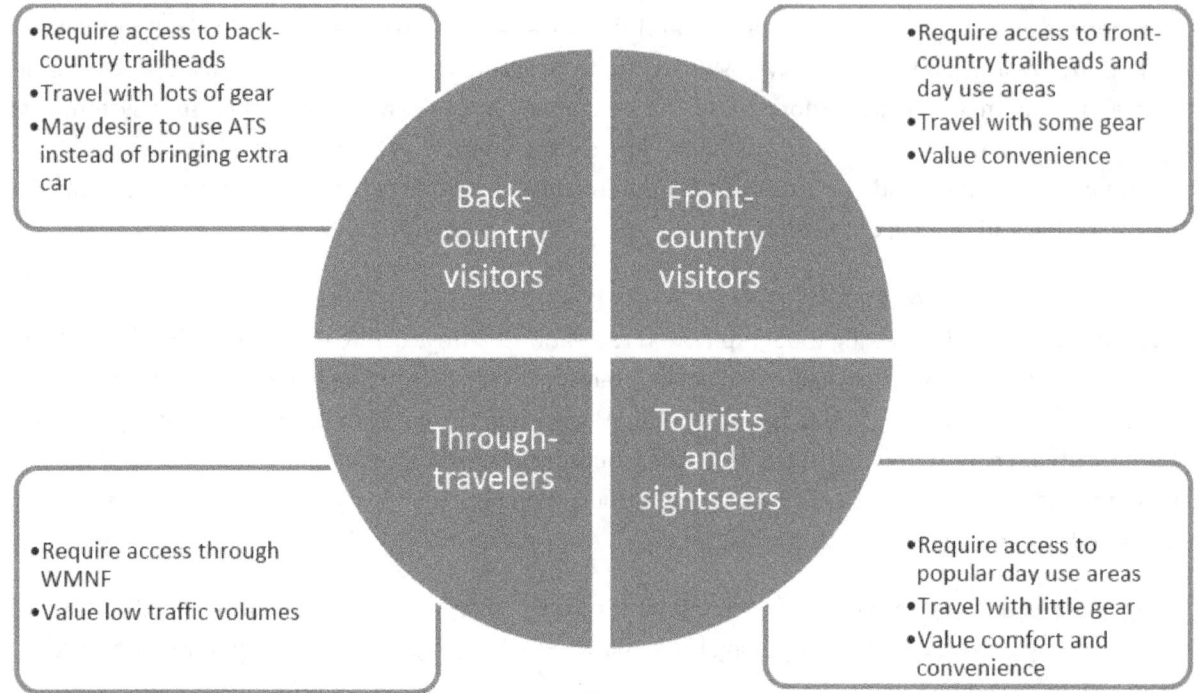

4.2 Visitor characteristics

The study team examined visitor characteristics using input from stakeholders, AMC, and USFS, as well as results from four surveys.

4.2.1 2010 WMNF National Visitor Use Monitoring results

The National Visitor Use Monitoring (NVUM) effort collects information on national forests and grasslands about visitor satisfaction and use, visitor group characteristics, distance traveled, visit types, frequency of visit, activities, economic activity, and satisfaction characteristics. The data collected for this report was from FY 2005. Data was collected again in 2010 but was not published in time to include in this report.

The NVUM survey interviewed 1,577 people. Of these, 62.3% were specifically recreating in the forest, while 29.5% were just passing through. As shown in Figure 12, while 19.3% of visitors are local (within 25 miles), all remaining visitors are from distances greater than 25 miles, with 32.5% coming from between 100 and 200 miles away, perhaps from the Boston metropolitan area. This distribution suggests potential demand for alternative transportation, not only in and around the WMNF, but also connecting to towns and cities in New England.

Figure 12 - Distance traveled to WMNF by visitors. Source: NVUM Results, 2005.

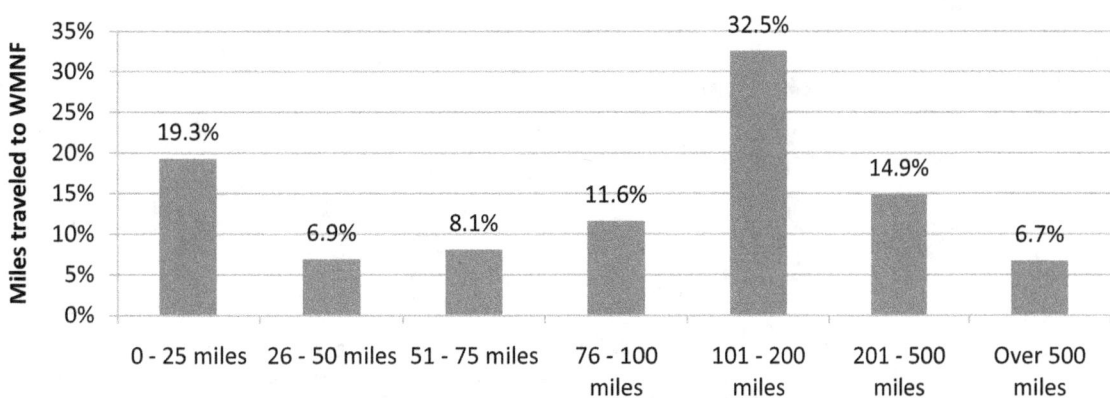

Over 48% of visitors report visiting WMNF between one and five times per year. Visitors reported their primary activities are downhill skiing/snowboarding, followed by hiking and walking, viewing natural scenery, cross country skiing or snow-shoeing, other non-motorized activities, or other, as shown in Figure 13.

Figure 13 - Percent of WMNF visitors who report primary activities. Source: NVUM Results, 2005.

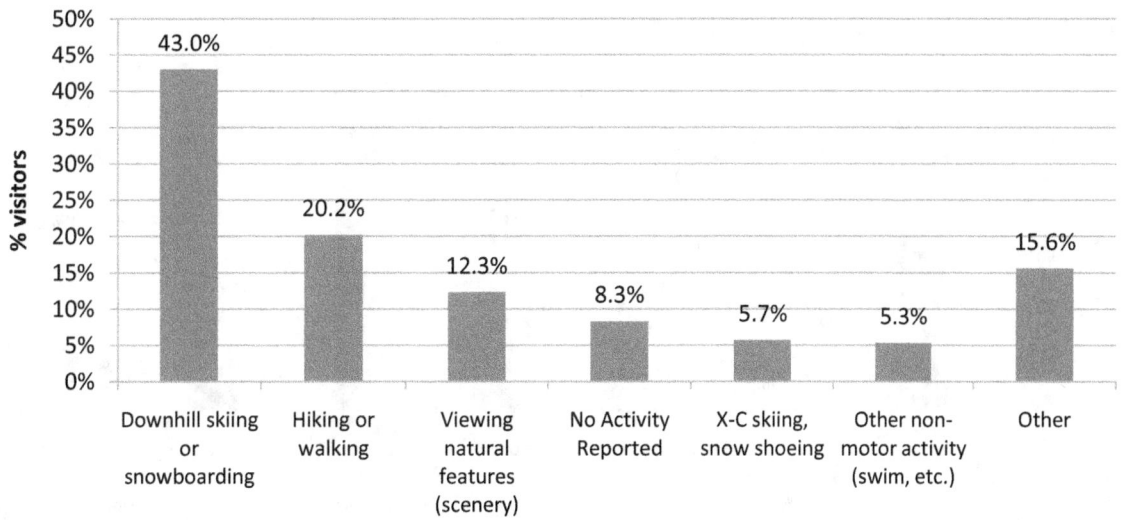

There is a great deal of overlap in WMNF visitor activities, as shown in Figure 13 and Figure 14. While only 12.3% of visitors enjoy viewing natural features as their primary activity, 55.5% of visitors engage in viewing natural features at WMNF. While 20.2% of visitors enjoy hiking or walking as their primary activity, 41.4% of visitors engage in hiking or walking at WMNF. Also shown in Figure 14, 61.0% of visitors like to relax at WMNF, and 17.3% of WMNF visitors drive for pleasure during their visits. These figures suggest that ATS that are convenient and contribute toward relaxing visits may be successful among some visitors, though other visitors may resist alternative transportation in favor of driving for pleasure.

Figure 14 - Percent of visitors who engage in activities in WMNF. Source: NVUM Results, 2005.

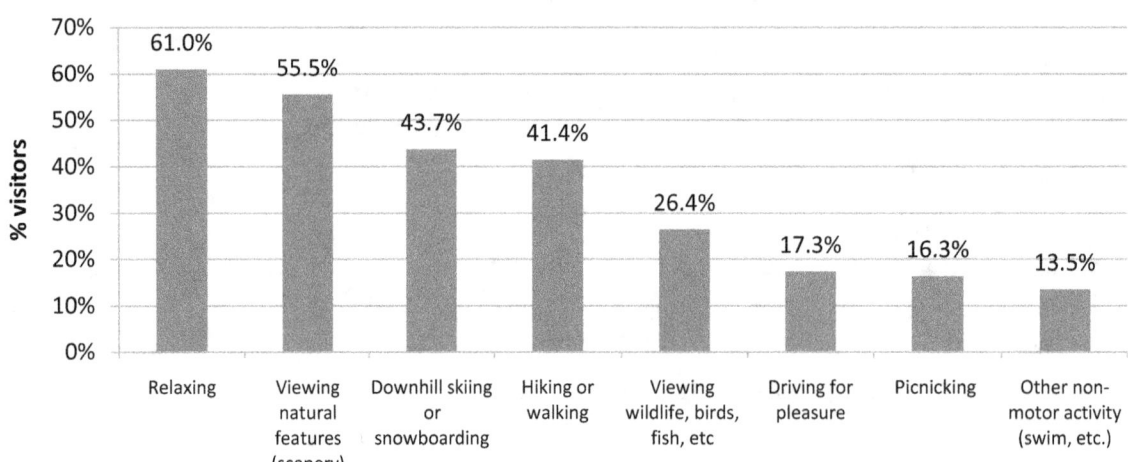

Over 24% of visitors to WMNF are locals making day trips, as shown in Figure 15. Almost 21% are non-locals making day trips, and over 28% are non-locals making overnight trips on which they stay in lodging off the forest. The latter statistic suggests there may be significant opportunities to work with the service sector, particularly hotels, when implementing ATS and visitor communications strategies. Only about 10% of visitors are non-locals who stay on the forest, either camping or in lodges or huts.

Figure 15 - Percent of visitors by trip type. Source: NVUM Results, 2005.

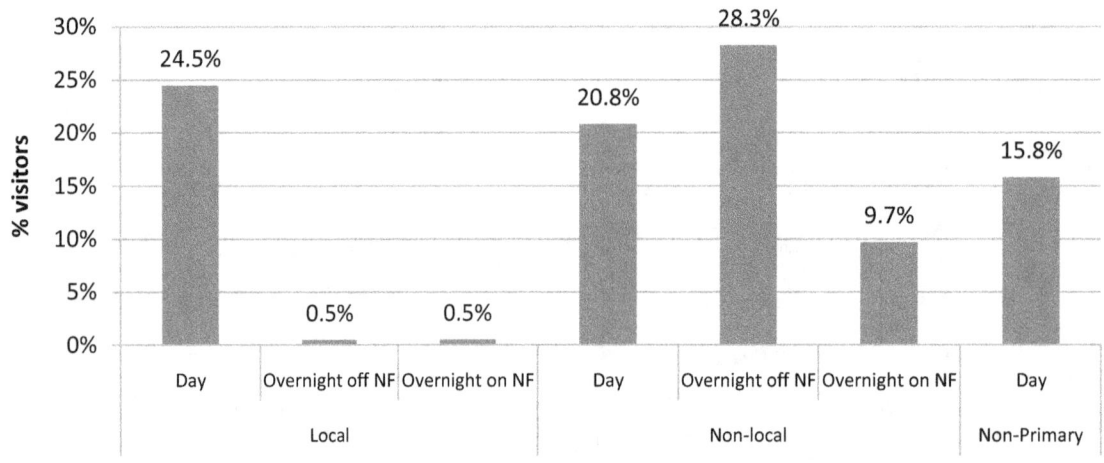

About 95% of visitors tended to be Very Satisfied or Somewhat Satisfied with road condition and sign adequacy at WMNF. About 86% of visitors rated road condition and sign adequacy an importance of 5 or a 4 out of 5. This suggests visitors place a high importance on traveler information and wayfinding, and any alternative transportation improvements should include these components.

4.2.2   AMC surveys

In 2010 AMC completed three survey efforts. One was a post-trip, web-based survey of guests of AMC White Mountain lodges and huts. The survey collected information from 824 traveler groups. Another was a survey of riders of its Hiker Shuttle riders during the summer season of 2010. Approximately 3000 people ride the shuttle each year, and 476 survey forms were received and tabulated. For the third survey, AMC worked with the USFS to add supplemental transportation-related questions to the 2010 WMNF NVUM study and augment the survey calendar with 16 additional dates at 8 sites that target backcountry users. Responses were received from 106 traveler groups. Several questions were included on all three surveys. Results of the surveys are described and compared below.

All three surveys found that cost and travel time / convenience were the most important factors when planning travel logistics, shown in Figure 16. Transporting gear, environmental impact, and social time were of more medium importance, while non-recreational activities were of much less importance. This suggests any alternative transportation system improvements must be cost-competitive compared with driving (for users) and convenient to users as well.

One interesting observation is that hikers who stayed at AMC huts placed a higher importance on transporting gear than did respondents from the other surveys. The reason for this is unknown, although perhaps hikers who stay in AMC huts pack more gear than hikers who ride the shuttle.

Figure 16 - AMC surveys: Factors most important when planning travel logistics.

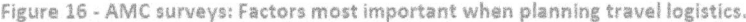

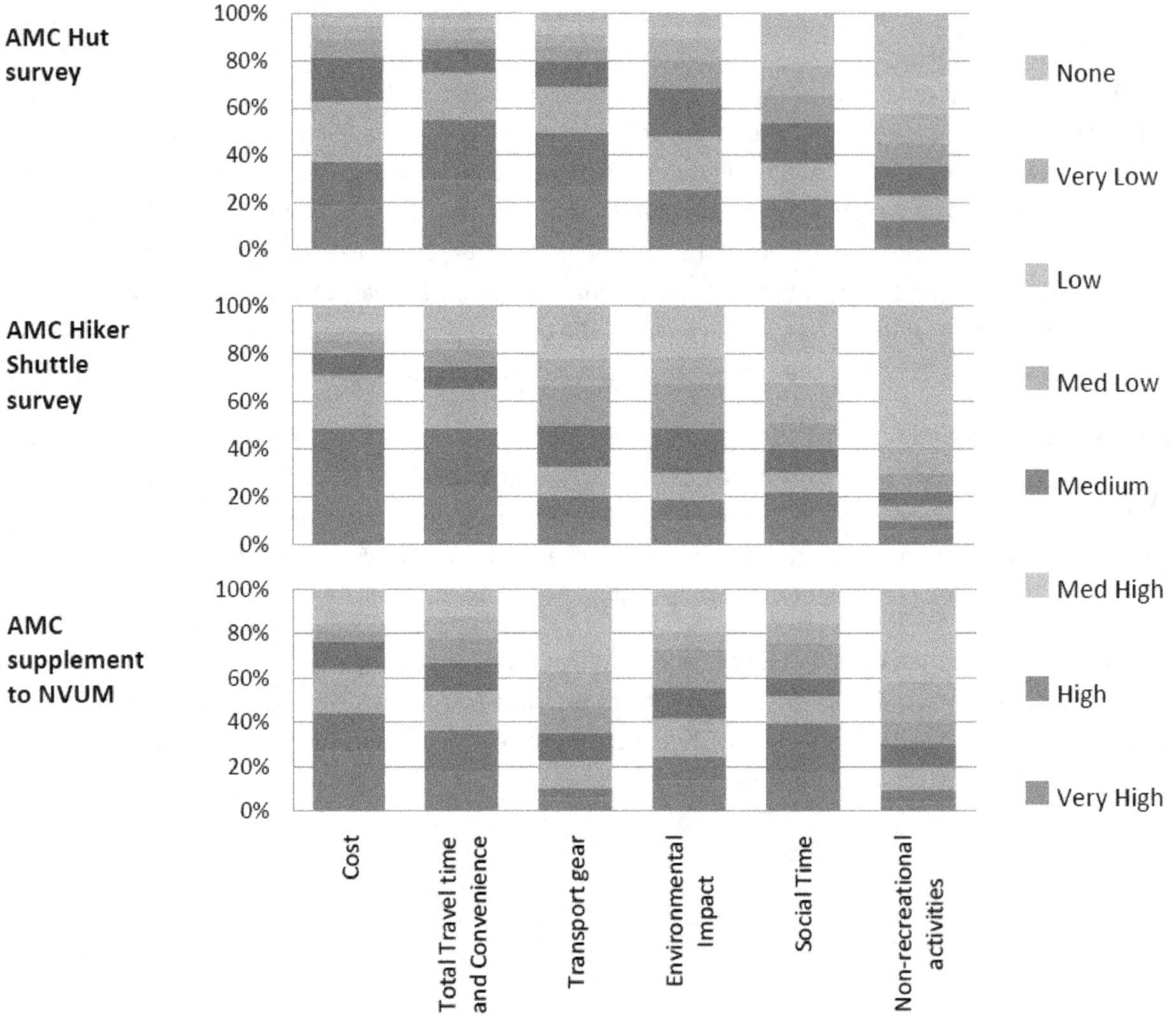

All three respondent groups reported that frequent and dependable service would be the most important factor above a lodging/meal package, discount coupons, or educational information, as shown in Figure 17. Respondents who stayed at AMC huts, however, were more likely than respondents of the other two surveys to consider transit if it were part of a lodging/meal. This is likely because these individuals are purchasing lodging and potentially meals from AMC already. These results generally suggest alternative transportation system improvements must be frequent and dependable.

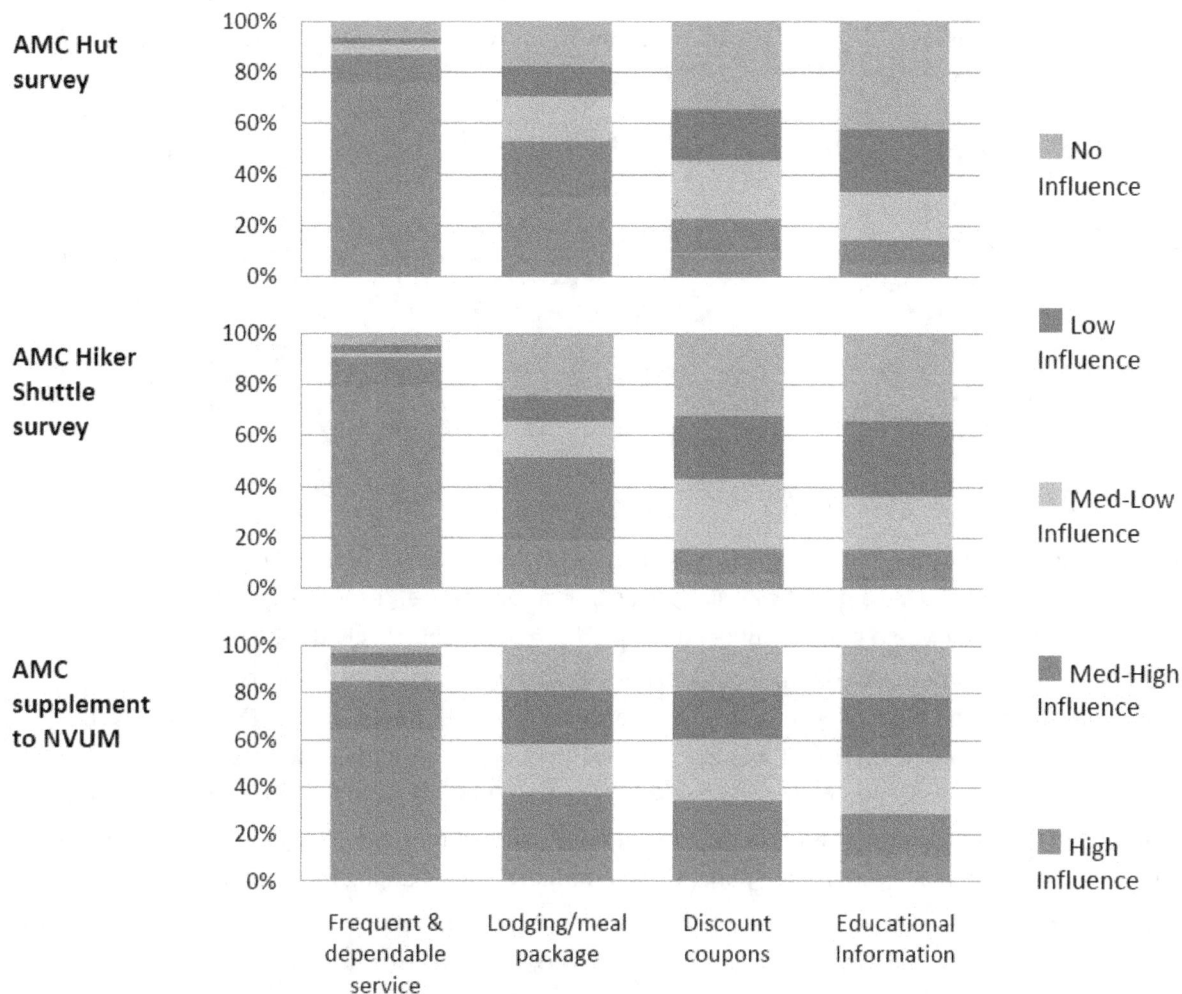

Respondents from all three surveys expressed a strong willingness to pay for a round-trip or daily transportation service from designated satellite lots to trailheads, attractions, and day use areas. As shown in Figure 18, current AMC shuttle riders said they would be willing to pay more than the respondents from the other two surveys. This is likely because current shuttle riders inherently value the shuttle, while other forest visitors may not have much shuttle experience. Very few visitors to AMC huts or riders of the AMC shuttle said they would not be willing to pay, while twelve percent of respondents to the NVUM survey said they would not be willing to pay. The reason for this may be related to branding. Consumers of AMC services may be more willing to pay for AMC services, while visitors unfamiliar with AMC may be less willing. In general, these results suggest that visitors to WMNF, particularly backcountry visitors with lots of gear, may be willing to pay for round-trip or daily transit service. Willingness to pay for one-way and/or single-leg trips, characteristic of more urban transit systems, is unclear.

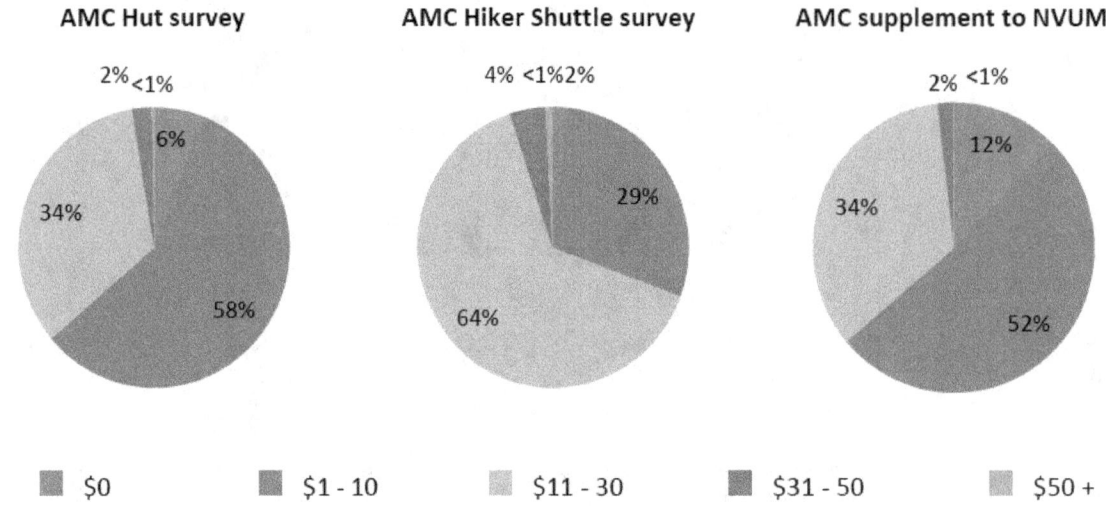

Figure 18 - AMC surveys: Willingness to pay for a round-trip or daily transportation service from designated satellite lots to trailheads, attractions, and day use areas.

When asked what actions taken to limit the number of private vehicles at recreational sites would most influence visitors to choose a publicly available transportation service, respondents from all three groups reported they would be most influenced by closure of parking lots with ticketed fines for illegal / overflow parking over increased or new parking fees or road closures or tolls, as shown Figure 19. Respondents from the Hiker Shuttle survey were least likely to be influenced by parking fees, likely because they were relying on transit already and were not concerned with siting cars and paying multiple parking fees[5]. On the other hand, guests of the AMC huts who did not take the shuttle may have siting cars at different locations in the forest and would be more influenced by parking fees. These results suggest that actively managing parking and enforcing illegal parking restrictions may incentivize visitors to take transit.

---

[5] Two or more hikers will often bring two cars to enable one-way hikes. They 'site' the first car at the destination of the hike and park the second at the origin of the hike. When the hike is completed, they use the first car to retrieve the second.

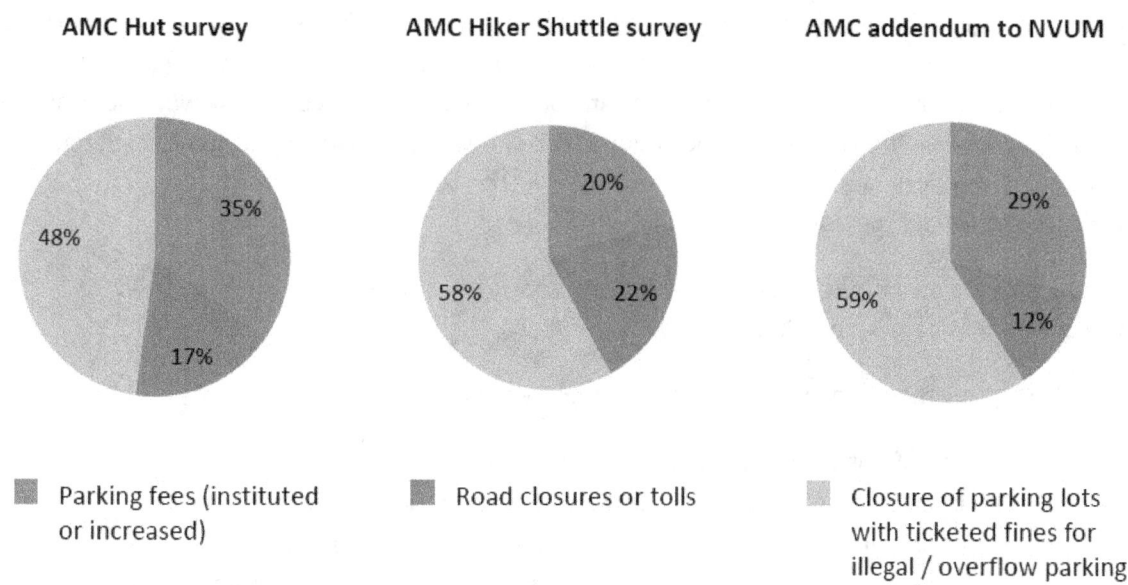

Figure 19 - AMC surveys: Actions designed to reduce private vehicle usage at recreational sites would most influence increased transit usage.

AMC Hut survey

48%
35%
17%

AMC Hiker Shuttle survey

20%
58%
22%

AMC addendum to NVUM

29%
59%
12%

■ Parking fees (instituted or increased)

■ Road closures or tolls

■ Closure of parking lots with ticketed fines for illegal / overflow parking

To recap, the three surveys yielded the following general results for those individuals surveyed:

- Cost, travel time, and convenience are the most important considerations when making travel plans;
- Frequent and dependable service are the most important positive factors in influencing respondents to ride transit;
- A significant majority of respondents are willing to pay between $11 and $30 for a round-trip or daily transportation service; and
- A significant majority of respondents would be influenced to ride transit if parking demand was managed and illegal / overflow parking were ticketed.

4.3 Stakeholder outreach

Stakeholder engagement with White Mountain region residents, and key local, state, and regional public, private, and non-profit sector organizations were crucial to identifying and developing the transportation issues and options found in *5 Alternative transportation issues and options*. Outreach activities supported the study goal of engaging stakeholders and explore partnership opportunities.

In-person workshops and a series of telephone discussions provided important information to the study team for understanding the transportation environment, expectations, and potential partnerships for ATS solutions in the White Mountains region. The three main outreach mechanisms included stakeholder engagement workshops, key informant discussions, and an Alternative Transportation Stakeholder Workshop. Additional documentation of these activities is provided in *Appendix B – Stakeholder outreach*.

4.3.1 Stakeholder engagement workshops

The study team led six stakeholder engagement workshops in July and August of 2010. Three were in-person meetings and three were conducted via conference call. The purpose of the workshops was to compile data on forest use patterns, attitudes toward transportation improvements, and acceptable transportation alternatives, and identify issues and options for further study. These workshops provided interaction between forest users and recreation service providers, and identified common themes, significant differences, and important insights regarding the public perception of transportation dynamics throughout the WMNF region.

Workshops were comprised of various regional transportation stakeholders. Approximately 30 individuals participated in the discussions.

The following key themes emerged during from these workshops:

- Knowledge of existing public transportation options is scant.
- Proper branding and education about transit is an important aspect of its use.
- A single, coordinated transit system may not be appropriate to serve all different user groups.
- Opportunities to improve existing alternative transportation infrastructure exist: bike paths, trails, and the potential to consolidate high use areas.
- The Forest Service should be a leading partner in transportation improvements.
- A champion is needed to drive alternative transportation and collaboration among partners in the region.

4.3.2 Key informant discussions

During August and September, 2010, the study team conducted seven telephone interviews with representatives from organizations that represent key public, private, and non-profit sector organizations responsible for, or with an interest in, transportation activities in the region. The purpose of these interviews was to seek feedback regarding the area's transportation strengths and weaknesses, current and planned projects, and challenges and opportunities for promoting alternative transportation in the region. The study team conducted discussions with individuals from the following organizations:

- New Hampshire Department of Resources and Economic Development (DRED)
- New Hampshire Department of Transportation, Bicycle and Pedestrian Program
- North Country Council
- North Country Transit (Tri-County CAP)
- White Mountain Attractions
- Concord Coach Lines
- C&J Bus Company

In addition to providing input on transportation strengths and weaknesses, key informants also expressed the following key themes, perceptions, and suggestions:

- While environmental benefits are important to North Country residents, economic realities have the greatest influence on daily decisions.

- There are opportunities to build on successes of existing projects, e.g. Franconia /Twin Mountain Trail, and the Notch-to-Notch Bike Path.
- Focused partnerships can improve: i) the existing wayfinding/signage in the WMNF; ii) the coordination or delivery of traveler information; iii) the use of Park & Ride lots to facilitate the use of transit; or iv) the expansion of existing transit services.
- There may be limited potential to mix human services transportation with recreational trips because of conflicting expectations among traveler groups.
- "Travel trainers" that use the economic costs of car ownership/insurance, etc. as a comparison to the cost of using transit service may encourage changes in travel behavior.
- Currently, transit systems in the WMNF area are fully utilizing their resources (vehicles, drivers, schedulers, phone operators, etc.) to operate the system. These systems may not be able to share vehicles or extend routes to the forest.
- Providing safe on-road cycling facilities remains a significant concern, but there are opportunities to create off-road multi-use paths that separate cyclists and pedestrians from vehicle travel.
- Cycling is allowed on virtually all roads, but multi-use paths are not accessible in winter months, November 15 through April 15.
- There may be opportunities to improve roadway signage to forewarn motorists that cyclists may be expected on certain roads.
- Education is needed to change the cultural attitude towards cyclists and the laws regarding cyclist use of the roads.
- There is a strong volunteer ethic in the WMNF region that could be leveraged to meet alternative transportation planning goals.
- There may be improved opportunities for ridesharing through the North Country Rideshare Program.
- Transportation planning activities should make use of alternative transportation project funding sources and schedules in the TRIP program, and state Transportation Enhancement (TE) funds.

4.3.3 Alternative Transportation Stakeholder Workshop

The Alternative Transportation Stakeholder Workshop held in December, 2010, was attended by 28 individuals primarily from the groups and agencies identified above. The purpose of the meeting was for the study team to present its initial findings to the stakeholder community and receive feedback

The study team used feedback from the stakeholder engagement workshops and key informant discussions held during the summer and fall to develop lists of area transportation strengths and weaknesses. These lists were verified at the Alternative Transportation Stakeholder Workshop. The region's transportation strengths include:

- AMC Hiker Shuttle
- Interstate bus connections to WMNF
- Regional and local, fixed route transit systems
- Multi-use paths

- State bicycle program
- Potential partners and stakeholders
- State Transportation Enhancement (TE) funds (roughly $6 million every two years)
- TRIP program funds

The region's transportation weaknesses include:

- Seasonal traffic and parking congestion
- Few incentives to discourage the use of cars
- No comprehensive, regional transit system
- Long distances between sites/attractions
- Potential unsafe conditions for cycling
- No central source of alternative transportation pre-trip traveler information
- Inadequate en-route signage and in wayfinding materials

The study team also presented draft lists of transportation issues and options and sought feedback from workshop participants. Results of the Alternative Transportation Stakeholder Workshop regarding the issues and options are included in *5 Alternative transportation issues and options*.

Confirming these strengths and weaknesses and issues and options with workshop participants allowed the study team to better consider transportation challenges, identify potential partnerships, and build solutions upon the areas inherent transportation assets, as described in *6 Transportation scenarios*.

4.4 Traffic analysis

Traffic counter data, usually presented as average daily traffic (ADT), provides important information with regard to understanding hourly, daily, and monthly transportation dynamics on segments of road. As part of this effort, the study team compiled and analyzed existing traffic counter data to determine if more traffic counter data collection is needed, and if so, where additional traffic counters should be installed.

4.4.1 Traffic counter analysis area

Roads in the study area, shown in Figure 2, are defined as follows (all are in New Hampshire unless otherwise noted):

- I-93 (between US-3 split and Plymouth)
- US-3, or Daniel Webster Highway (between I-93 and US-302)
- US-302, or Crawford Notch Road (between US-3 and NH-16/US-302)
- NH-16/US-302 or White Mountain Highway (between US-302 and NH-112)
- NH-112, or Kancamagus Highway (between NH-16/US-302 and I-93)
- Bear Notch Road (between US-302 and NH-112)
- NH-49 from Campton to Waterville Valley
- NH 112 from Woodstock to Bath
- NH-175 from Holderness to Woodstock

- NH-110 from Groveton to Berlin
- US-3 from Plymouth to Twin Mountain
- NH-16 from West Ossipee to Berlin
- NH-3A/NH-25 from Wentworth to Plymouth
- NH-118 from Warren to North Woodstock
- US-2 from Lancaster to Bethel, ME
- US-302 from Bethlehem to Fryeburg, ME
- NH-113/ME-113 from Conway to Gilead, ME

4.4.2 Available data

New Hampshire Department of Transportation (NHDOT) has the following datasets publicly available in portable document format (PDF) via its website and in Excel format by request:

- **Traffic Volume Reports by County and Town**– Listed by county and town, this dataset contains Annual Daily Traffic (ADT) figures for road segments organized by county, then town. ADT is listed for years from 2001 to 2008, but not every year. This data was recorded by temporary traffic recorders, the same as in Traffic Volume Reports by Route (below).
- **Traffic Volume Reports by Route** – Listed by route, this dataset contains ADT figures for road segments organized by route. ADT is listed for years from 2001 to 2008, but not every year. This data was recorded by temporary traffic recorders, the same as in Traffic Volume Reports by County and Town (above).
- **Traffic Volume Reports, 200 Highest Hours** – This dataset contains the 200 most congested hours registered for each of the permanent automatic traffic recorders (see Automatic Traffic Recorder Reports below) in New Hampshire. Data files are organized by year from 1993 to 2008. The data for each counter is reported as hourly volume for one or both directions for each road segment.
- **Automatic Traffic Recorder Reports** – This dataset contains month on month ADT comparisons for each of New Hampshire's permanent automatic traffic recorders (the same recorders as from Traffic Volume Reports, 200 Highest Hours) from 2003 to 2009. The number of permanent automatic traffic recorders has changed over time. As of August 2009, there were 61 permanent automatic traffic recorders. Data files are organized by year and month. Six permanent traffic counters are located in the New Hampshire study area: Bartlett, Campton, Jefferson, Lincoln, Ossipee, and Rumney.
- **Traffic Detail Sheets** – This dataset contains hourly volumes from temporary traffic recorders for periods of up to seven days. Data is organized by county, town, and then year. Hourly counts go back as far as 1994 but were not observed in each year in each location. Sample counts were made in the WMNF study area, however these counts are for seven day periods once a year, and do not provide insight into weekly, monthly, or seasonal trends.

Maine DOT provided the following data, both by request and through their website[6]:

---

[6] http://www.state.me.us/mdot/traffic-counts/traffic-monitoring.php

- **Permanent automatic traffic recorder data for Bethel location.** This Excel spreadsheet contains daily traffic counts for the year 2008 at the permanent traffic recorder on US 2 north of Bethel Rd. in Bethel.
- **Temporary traffic recorder locations for all traffic counts dating to 1978.** This ArcGIS shapefile details locations of each temporary traffic recorder used by Maine DOT dating back to 1978. The shapefile includes ADT figures for each recording instance. Table 1 includes locations that have recorded a traffic count since 2004 and are considered active; locations that have not recorded a traffic count since 2004 are excluded.
- **2008 Traffic Count Book.** This dataset contains ADT figures from temporary and permanent traffic recorders between 2004-2008, organized by county and town.
- **ADT data along Maine public road segments.** This ArcGIS shapefile features ADT figures along Maine public road segments from the time of the last count, as well as basic road information including route numbers, speed limits, and jurisdiction. Almost all ADT figures were recorded between 2004 and 2008.

Locations of temporary (and permanent) traffic counters within the study area and ADT for many road segments are shown in Figure 20. Temporary traffic count data provides a snapshot of transportation activity at any given time, but because of the short periods for which ADT was recorded at these locations, hourly, weekly, monthly, and seasonal variation is unknown on these segments. Thus the temporary traffic counter information is useful for estimating overall vehicular volume for the forest, but not usage peaks and year-round traffic patterns at matched times and paired locations along key corridors, which can be used to estimate commuting versus visitor travel.

Figure 20 - Locations of temporary and permanent counters and average daily traffic on study area roads.

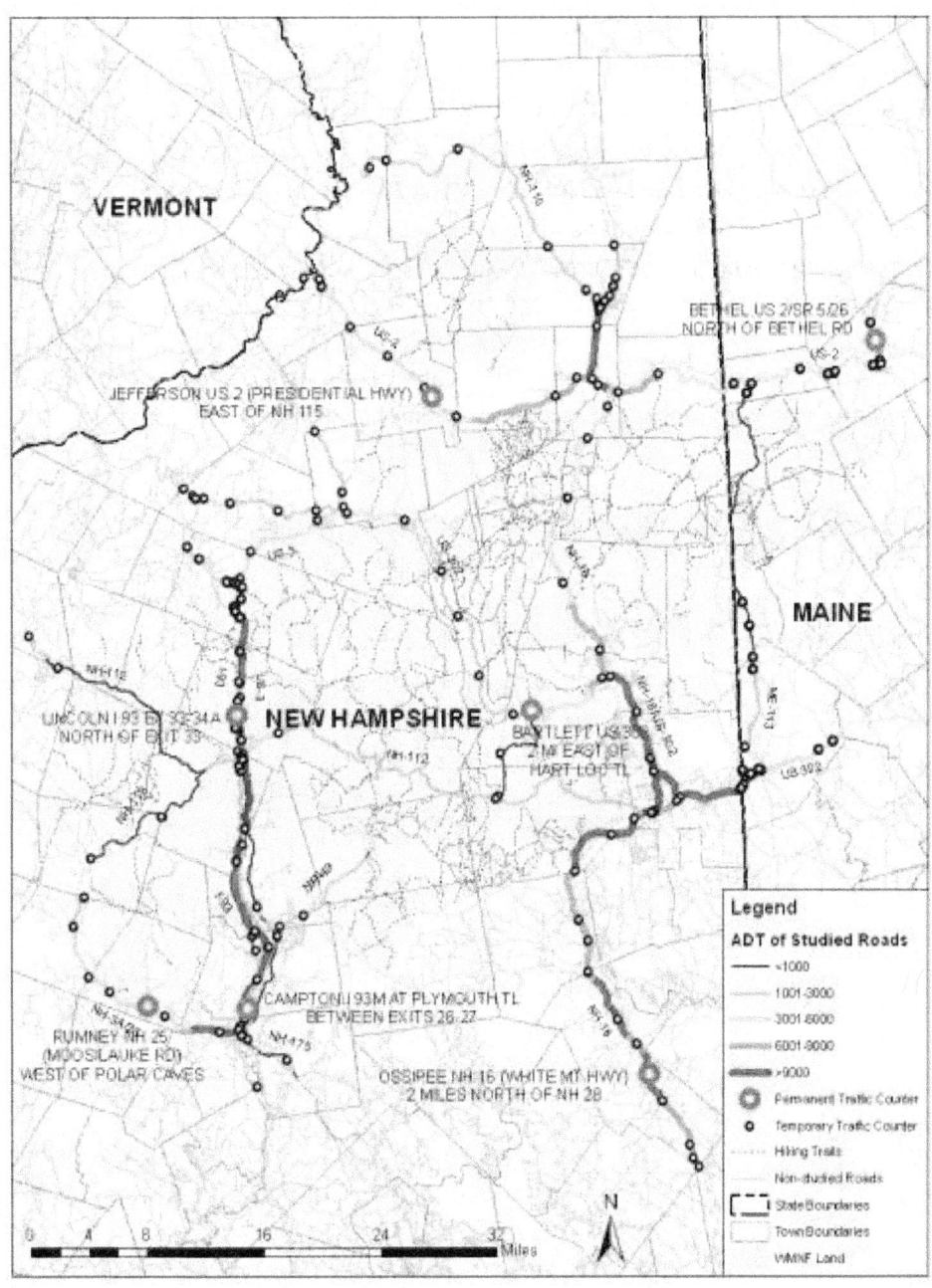

4.4.3 Analysis of data from permanent counters

In order to understand spatial and temporal trends, data were analyzed from the following seven permanent traffic counters located in the study area:

- **BARTLETT 2 MI E OF HARTS LOC TL**, recording both east and westbound traffic hourly on US-302 near Bartlett, two miles east of Hart's Location town line, 1999-2008;
- **BETHEL US 2/SR 5/26 NORTH OF BETHEL RD**, recording both north and southbound traffic daily on US 2 near Bethel, 2008;
- **CAMPTON- I-93 AT PLYMOUTH TL BETWEEN EXITS 26-27**, recording both north and southbound traffic hourly on I-93, 2008;
- **JEFFERSON- US 2 (PRESIDENTIAL HWY) EAST OF NH 115**, recording both east and westbound traffic hourly on US 2, 2008;
- **LINCOLN- I-93 AT CROSSOVER AT MILEPOST 103.1 BETWEEN EXIT 33 & 34A**, recording both north and southbound traffic hourly on I-93, 2008;
- **OSSIPEE- NH 16 (WHITE MT HWY) 2 MILES NORTH OF NH 28**, recording both north and southbound traffic hourly on NH 16, 2008; and
- **RUMNEY- NH 25 (MOOSILAUKE RD) WEST OF POLAR CAVES**, recording both north and southbound traffic hourly on NH 25, 2008.

Because 2008 traffic data was available from all seven traffic counters, this analysis focuses on 2008. All permanent counters in New Hampshire report hourly counts, while the Bethel, Maine, counter reports daily.

Figure 21 shows the number of hours counted by each traffic counter for each month during 2008. A month with 30 days consists of 720 hours. Counters in Bartlett, Bethel[7], Campton, and Lincoln were operational for most of the year. The counter in Jefferson was out of order for significant periods of time during January, February, March, September, and December. The counter in Ossipee was out of order during part of January and December. The counter in Rumney was out of order for significant periods in June and July. The counter in Lincoln was out of order for roughly half of December. Additional years of data for these counters would improve the quality of results in these areas.

---

[7] Operational hours for Bethel were estimated based on the number of operational days. Days for which counts were not provided by Maine DOT were assumed to be non-operational for 24 hours.

Figure 21 - Number of hours counted by month, 2008.

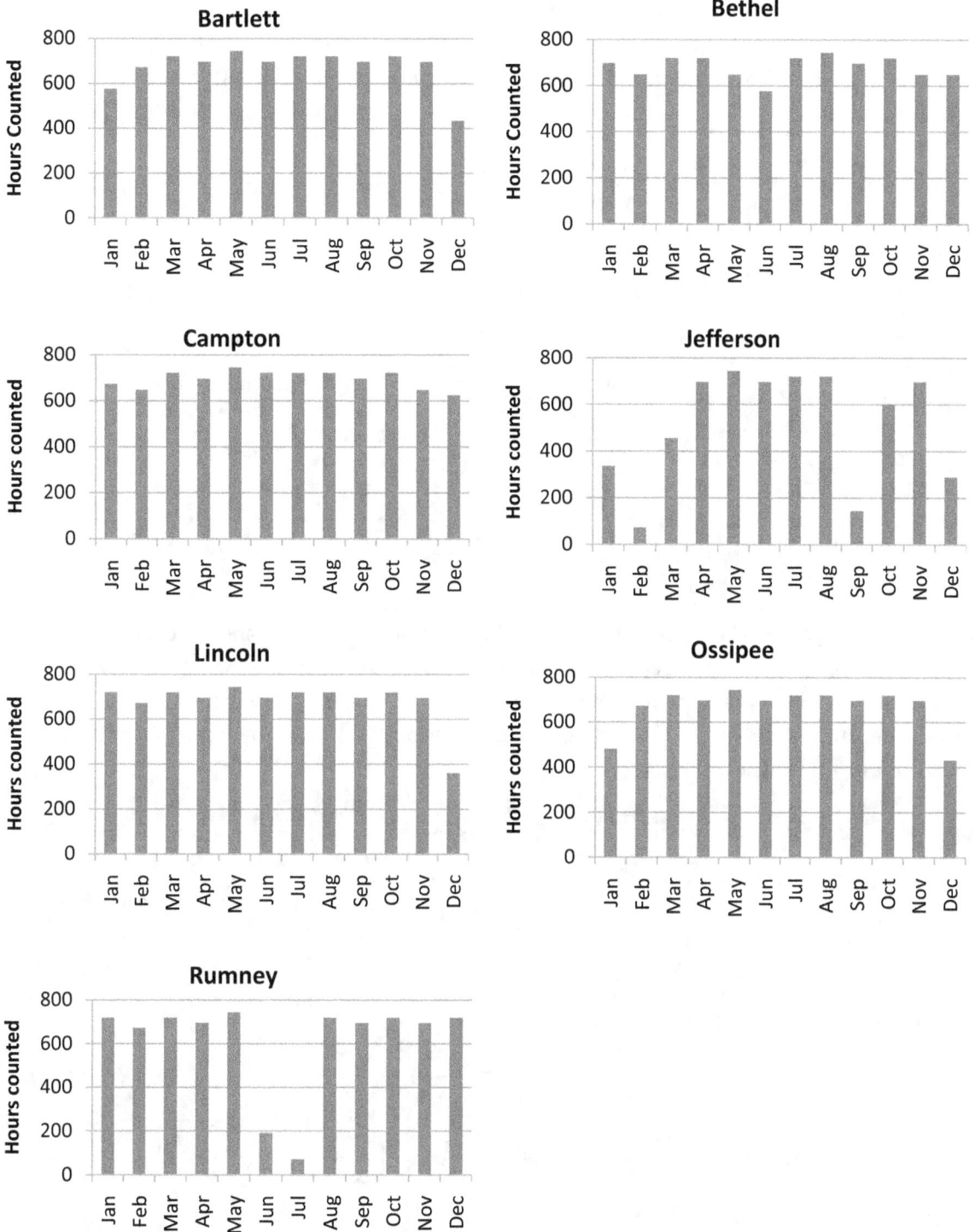

Figure 22 shows average hourly volume by month during 2008 for all counters except Bethel, which did not report hourly counts. Average hourly volume for all other counters peaks in July and August in the summer, and again slightly in October, likely due to visitors coming to see fall foliage. The counters in Campton, Ossipee, and Lincoln (located on I-93, NH-16, and I-93 respectively) register higher average hourly volume than the counters located in Rumney and Jefferson (located on NH 25 and US 2, respectively).

Figure 22 - Average hourly volume, bi-directional traffic, 2008. Data unavailable for Bethel.

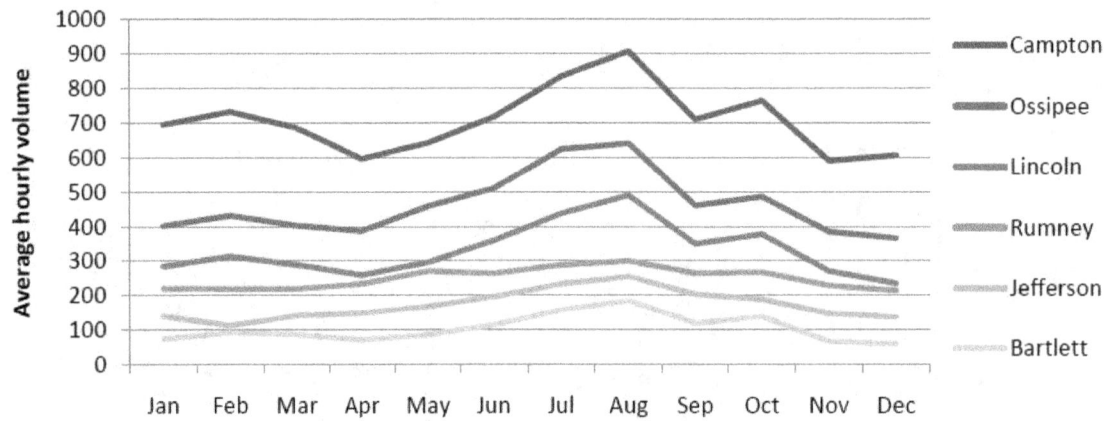

Figure 23 shows average ADT by type of day during 2008. Campton, Ossipee, and Lincoln have higher volumes on Friday, Saturday, and Sunday than on weekdays, suggesting these roads support more recreational travel on weekends than commuter traffic during the week. Daily patterns in Rumney, Jefferson, Bethel, and Bartlett are less distinguished. For all locations, weekday traffic volumes on Monday through Thursday are similar.

Figure 23 - ADT by day of week, bi-directional traffic, 2008.

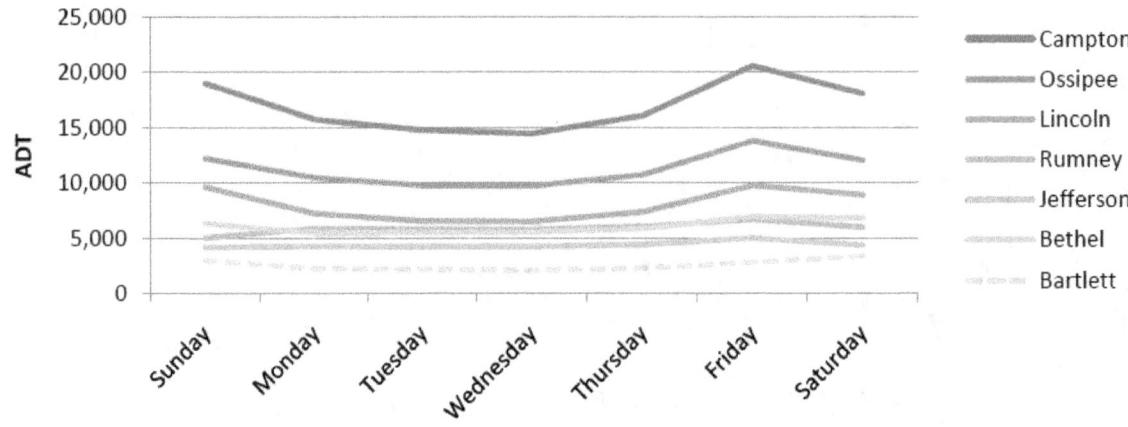

Figure 24 shows average ADT by type of day and month during 2008. The highest ADT occurs during July and August. At Bartlett, Campton, Lincoln, and Rumney, Saturday and Sunday volumes tend to be higher than weekdays throughout the year. These areas likely support more discretionary and recreational travel than commuter traffic. Jefferson and Ossipee see more weekday traffic than Saturday and Sunday traffic, suggesting these roads are used more for commuting and work travel during the week. Bethel experiences a mixture, depending on the time of the year. Winter, peak summer, and peak fall months in Bethel see more Saturday and Sunday traffic than weekday traffic, while non-peak months have more weekday traffic.

Figure 24 - Summary of ADT reported by month and type of day, bi-directional traffic, 2008.

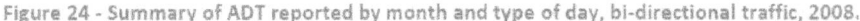

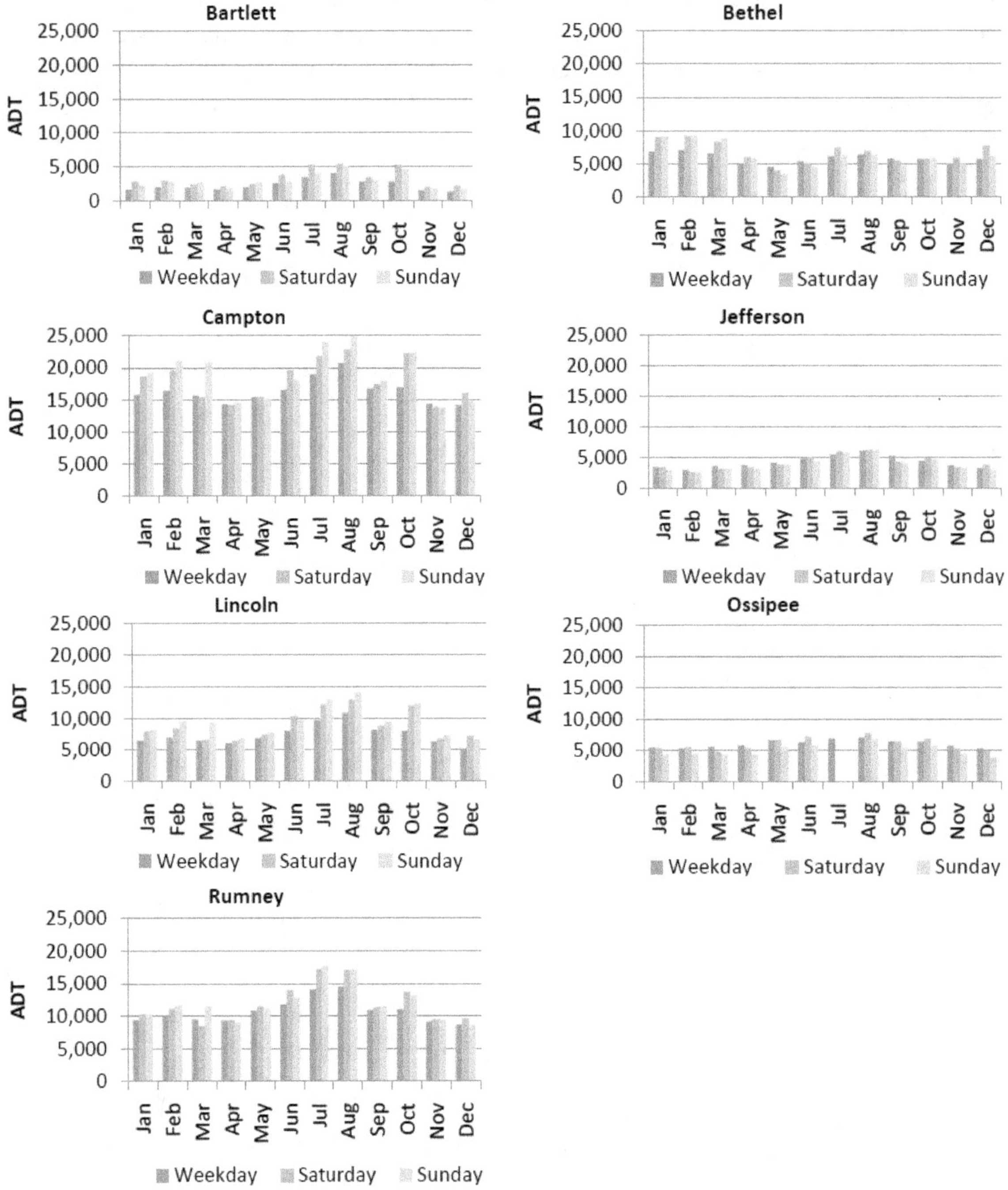

Figure 25 shows hourly volume by time of day, 2008. Hourly counts were not available for Bethel. At all six sites, weekend volume are greater than weekday volume between 8:00am and 10:00pm. Weekday volume is greater than weekend volume between 4:00am and 8:00am. Traffic on weekends peaks in the morning around 11:00am and in the afternoon around 3:00pm. Traffic on weekdays rises sharply in the morning until leveling off around 7:00am. Weekday traffic rises sharply again around 2:00pm, peaks around 4:00pm, and declines sharply until morning.

Figure 25 - Summary of ADT reported by month, type of day, and time of day bi-directional traffic, 2008.

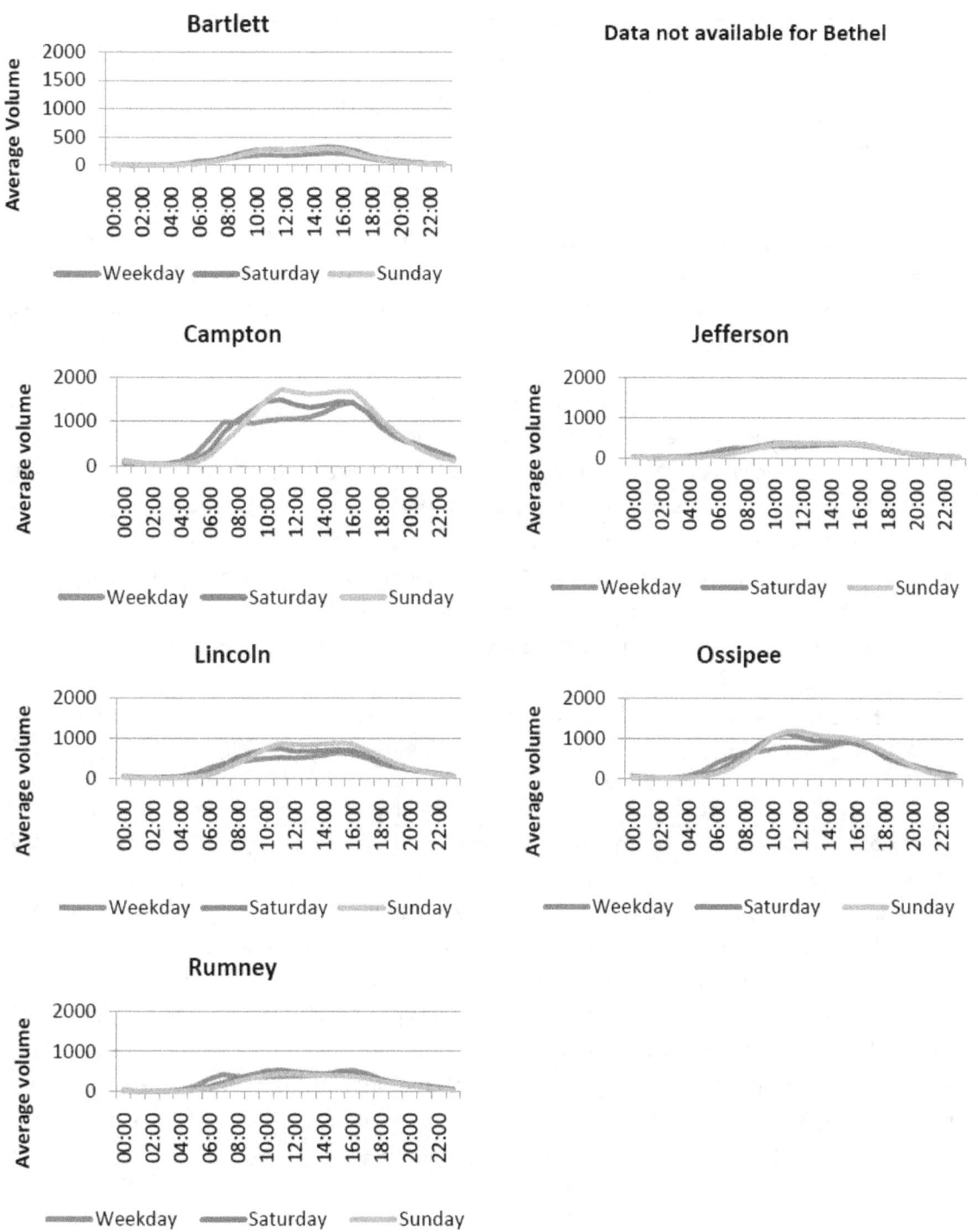

4.4.4 Key findings

Data from the seven permanent traffic counters suggest general spatial and temporal travel patterns in the study area. In particular, peak travel times are as follows:

- The months of July, August, and October;
- Weekends, which on a daily basis account for more travel than weekdays, suggesting that recreational travel accounts for a significant portion of total travel in the area; and in particular
- Late weekend mornings through early afternoons, 10AM – 3PM.

However, most of these counters are located outside of the WMNF and collect a great deal of data about non-recreationalist road users.

Permanent traffic counters should be installed in key corridors in the forest, specifically outside of developed areas which may generate a large proportion of local, non-recreational trips. After reviewing the traffic analysis presented in this memo, the study team suggested the following locations shown in Figure 26, for additional permanent traffic counters:

- **Kancamagus Highway at Lincoln Woods Visitor Center**. This location is within the WMNF and would capture visitation at a popular trailhead facility.
- **Kancamagus Highway at Dugway Road near Albany covered bridge**. This location is within the WMNF and will capture visitation at a popular day use area that includes two campgrounds, a trailhead, a picnic/interpretive area, and a historic site.
- **North of Jackson on Rt 16 at the Rocky Branch trailhead parking facility**. This location is sufficiently north of commercial and residential to filter out local traffic.
- **South of Gorham on Rt 16 at Dolly Copp Road**. This location is within the WMNF and will capture visitation to two campgrounds, a day use area, and a trailhead.
- **East of Carroll on Rt 302 at Mount Clinton Road**. This location is sufficiently south of Bretton Woods and commercial, retail, and ski-related development to filter out local traffic.

The installation of, and data collection and processing from, these new permanent traffic counters should be coordinated with New Hampshire and Maine DOTs. The availability of this data will help the departments of transportation and other organizations better understand transportation dynamics in the forest and states. In addition, combining WMNF specific traffic counter data with analysis of WMNF recreational sites, as outlined in *4.8 WMNF recreational infrastructure analysis*, will aid Forest Service staff in assessing visitor use patterns and possible non-motorized improvements. For example, revealing accurate seasonal increase in ADT on specific road segments provides WMNF managers with the ability to predict where traffic congestion may occur. In turn, this information combined with use-levels at recreational sites throughout the WMNF can be used to appropriately plan transit routes and boarding/alighting locations. The same information could be used to plan for bicycle or pedestrian infrastructure planning.

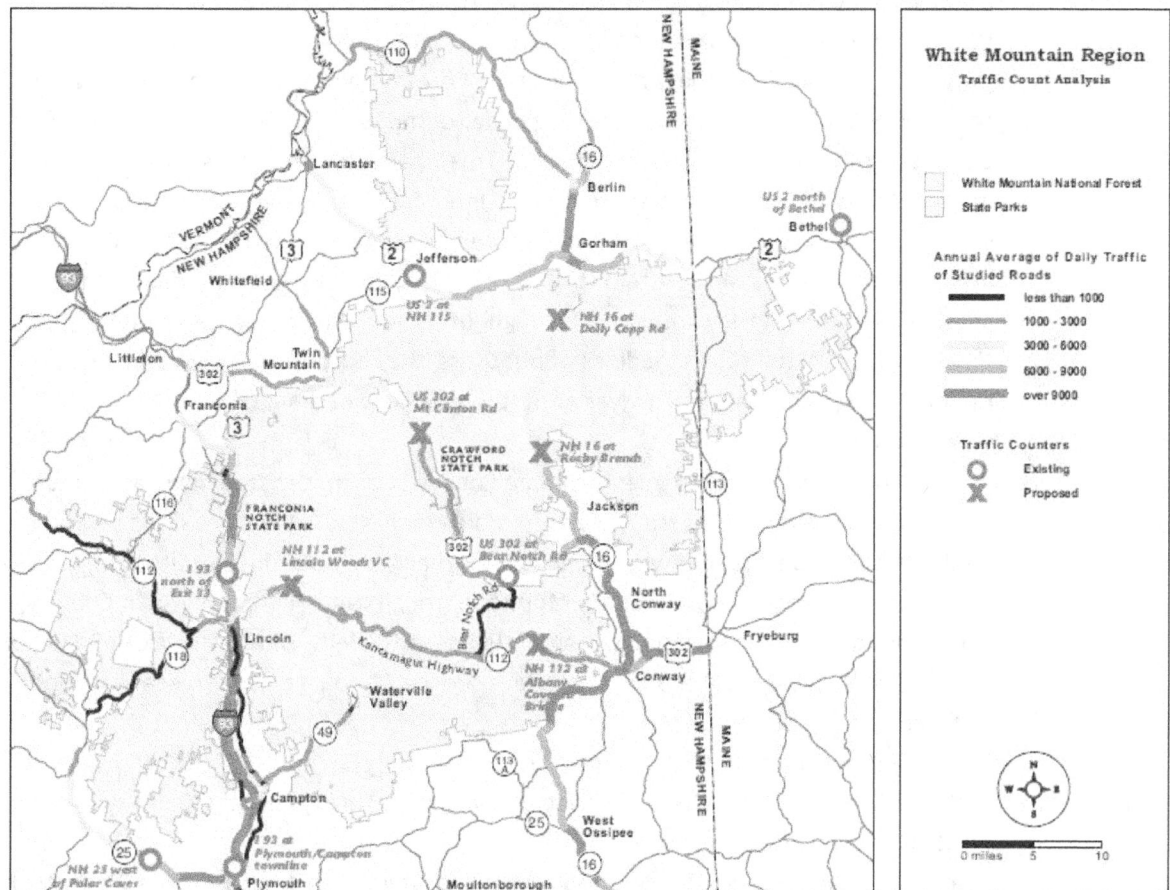

4.5 Transit systems and gaps

The study team inventoried existing transit systems in the study area, identified gaps among existing systems, and documented challenges to providing transit to locations in the WMNF.

4.5.1 Transit inventory

Area transit providers may be broken into three categories: public transit, private transportation, and tourism-related. A map of the fixed-route services is provided in Figure 27.

- Public transit
  - **North Country Transit** is a branch of the Tri-County Community Action Program (Tri-County CAP), and serves Berlin/Gorham, Lancaster, and Northern Coos County. Clients range from senior citizens and people with disabilities to children in need of a ride to the mall. Current services include the **Berlin/Gorham flexible route trolley** allowing route deviations up to a ¼ mile for call-ahead scheduled stops. The **Tri-Town bus** services the towns of Lancaster, Whitefield, and Littleton. A recent grant from the American Recovery and Reinvestment to the NH DOT has enabled creation of **Carroll County**

Transit which provides commuter shuttles from West Ossipee to Laconia and West Ossipee to Wolfboro and a demand response service from Conway to Wolfboro .

- o **White Mountain Transit Authority** runs a village taxi in and around Conway, and provides seasonal scenic tours throughout the Conway/Jackson/Mt. Washington area.
- o The **AMC Hiker Shuttle** serves the northern tier of the WMNF. Open to members of the public and offering discounted fares for AMC members, this seasonal shuttle stops at major trailheads along Routes 16, 302, 3 and Interstate-93. The AMC shuttle is successful both in terms of its cost recovery and its utility provided to riders. AMC attributes the success of its system to several factors, namely that AMC markets the availability of the shuttle extensively throughout its hut system and the shuttle system is timed specifically to fit the schedules of hut users (the shuttle departs for trailheads right after hut breakfasts and arrives at huts in time for hut dinners).

- Private transportation
  - o Privately operated bus companies including **Concord Coach, C+J Trailways, and Peter Pan** provide access from Massachusetts to Maine with New Hampshire stops in: Berlin, Center Harbor, Concord, Conway, Franconia, Gorham, Jackson, Lincoln, Littleton, Londonderry, Manchester, Meredith, Moultonborough, New Hampton, North Conway, North Londonderry, Pinkham Notch (AMC), Plymouth, Salem, Tilton, and West Ossipee.
  - o **Dave's Taxi** is based in Littleton and provides service 24 hours a day for local and long distance transportation.
  - o **EZ Taxi** is based in the Berlin/Gorham area.
  - o **Fast Taxi Service** provides local and long distance rides throughout the Conway area for residents and tourists.
  - o The **Shuttle Connection of North Woodstock** is located in the Lincoln/North Woodstock area. Providing transportation to hikers, it accesses many of the major trailheads in the southern section of the WMNF with routes along: Tripoli Rd., Franconia Notch, Kancamagus Highway 112 East, Lost River Road 112 West, Warren Mountain Road 118, Rte. 3 North to Twin Mountain, Top of Crawford Notch, In Crawford Notch, From Rte. 115 Gorham, and Pinkham Notch.

- Tourism-related providers
  - o The **Mount Washington Hotel** in Bretton Woods, the **Mountain View Grand Hotel** in Whitefield, and the **BALSAMS Resort** in Dixville Notch each provide guest access to their shuttle systems **which** connect to major shopping and recreation centers throughout the region.
  - o **Loon Mountain** in Lincoln, **Cannon Mountain** in the Franconia Notch State Park, **Attitash Ski Resort** in Bartlett, **Bretton** Woods at the base of Mount Washington, and the **Waterville Valley Resort** in Waterville Valley each provide access to shuttle buses for visitors and employees throughout the winter season.

Figure 27 - Fixed route transit services in the study area.

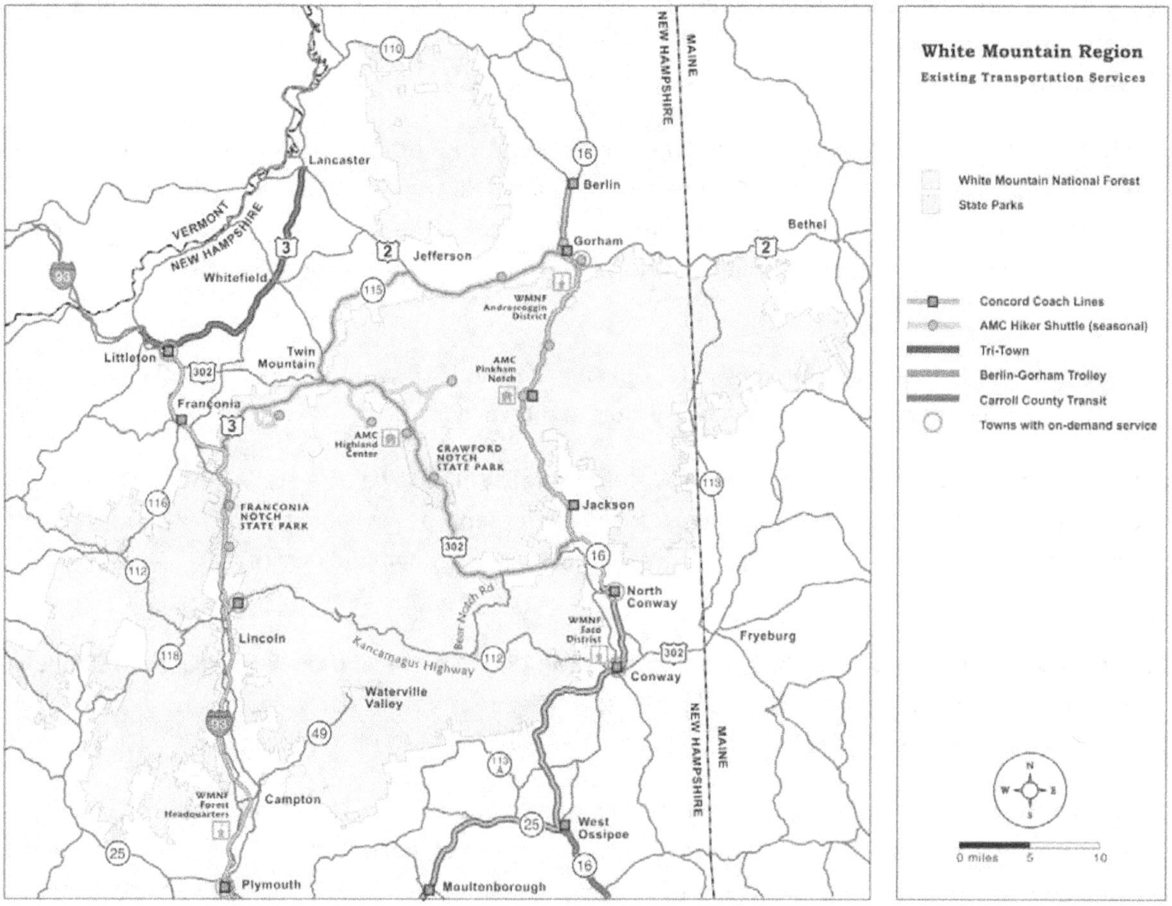

4.5.2 Transit gaps

The transit environment in the WMNF region is characterized by both transit service gaps and transit schedule gaps. The former indicates a lack of a physical service between locations, while the latter implies a lack of coordinated schedules between services, which make transfers from location to location on multiple transit lines difficult or improbable. Solutions to scheduling gaps may be easier to resolve than spatial gaps in transit service because amending schedule times may not require additional resources like employees, vehicles, and fuel. The spatial and schedule transit gaps described below and shown in Figure 28 are the basis for several of the transit issues described in *5.1 Alternative transportation issues*.

4.5.2.1 Transit service gaps

Lack of local transit service to recreational destinations, including Franconia Notch State Park. The lack of local transit options among key recreation destinations and significant tourist lodging and residential areas in the WMNF represents significant transit service gaps. The towns of Lincoln, Franconia, Conway, and North Conway have no transit connections with Franconia State Park, the Kancamagus Highway, and other popular recreation destinations, like Lincoln Woods. For example, Concord Coach Lines serves both Lincoln and Franconia but nothing in between, and the AMC Hiker Shuttle serves two points along the corridor, but does not serve either town. As a result, no common transit service node exists between these two services in this north-south corridor. Additionally, Lincoln is a large population center with several visitor accommodations and amenities. Tourists and residents there have no public transportation option to Franconia Notch State Park.

Similarly, the towns of Conway and North Conway are popular tourist destinations. Concord Coach Lines serves both Conway and North Conway, and Carroll County Transit provides service to or from communities south or North Conway. The nearest AMC Hiker Shuttle stop is located roughly five miles north of North Conway. Therefore, visitors in North Conway have no connection to this popular hiker shuttle.

Finally, no transit service exists on Route 112, the Kancamagus Highway, to connect Lincoln and Conway, though there are many popular trailheads and sites in this corridor.

No transit service connects Plymouth with Waterville Valley. The town of Waterville Valley is a recreational destination but has no regional transportation service that connects with Plymouth (which is served by Concord Coach Lines). Visitors must rely on taxi or on-demand services.

4.5.2.2 Transit schedule gaps
Lack of coordinated scheduled stops between the AMC Hiker Shuttle and the Berlin/Gorham Trolley. The Berlin/Gorham Trolley operates on a limited schedule, does not support direct transfers with Concord Coach Lines, and provides limited connections with the AMC Hiker Shuttle.

Lack of coordinated schedule/transit transfers in Littleton between Tri-Town and Concord Coach Lines. Both Concord Coach Lines and the Tri-Town bus serve the town of Littleton. However, to connect between the Tri Town bus and the Concord Coach Lines requires an early morning demand service request to the Tri-Town bus, making this connection inconvenient for travelers.

Lack of coordinated schedule/transit transfers in Pinkham Notch between AMC Hiker Shuttle and Concord Coach Lines. Pinkham Notch Visitor Center has a common transit location node with both the Concord Coach Lines and the AMC Hiker Shuttle. However, a transfer between the services would require an overnight stay in Pinkham Notch because the only Concord Coach southbound departure leaves Pinkham at 8:07 AM, and the only Concord Coach PM northbound arrives at Pinkham at 9:10 PM.

Figure 28 - Transit gaps in the study area.

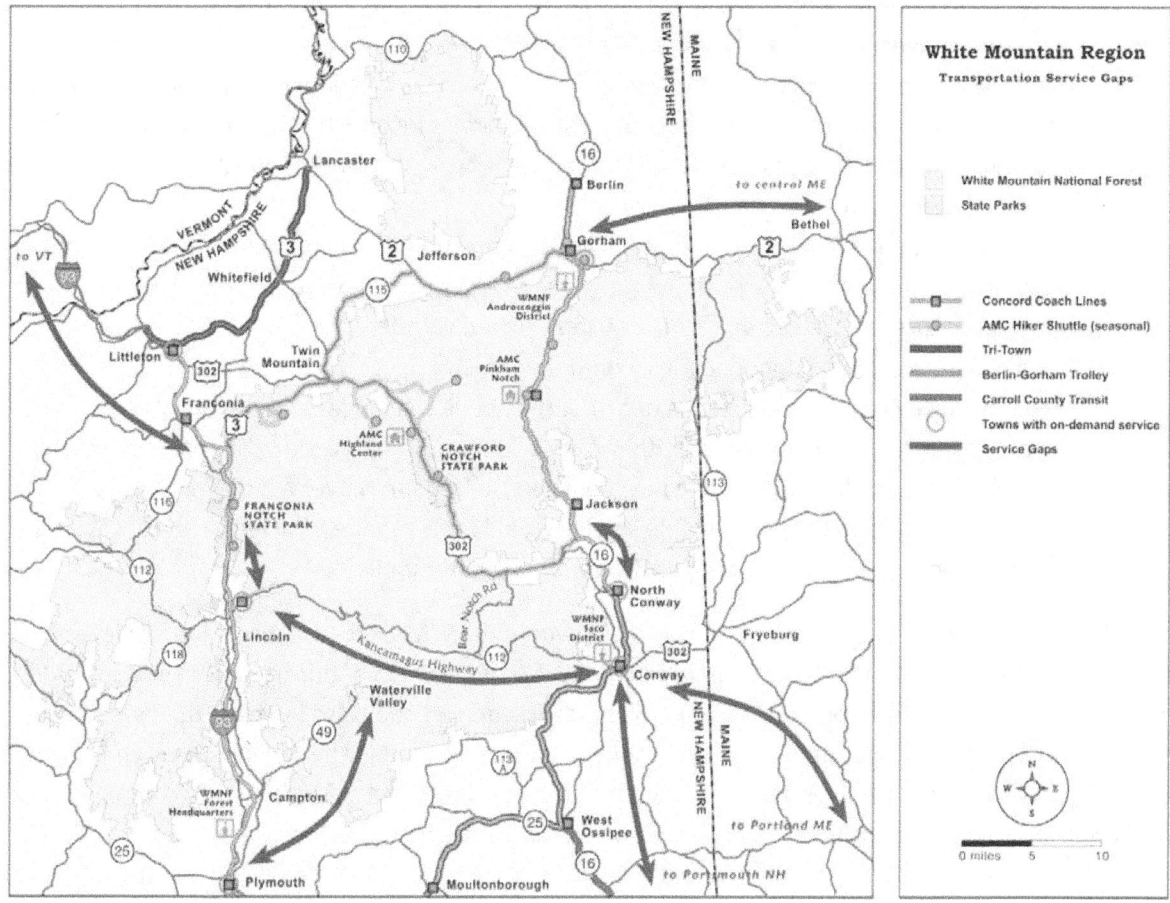

4.5.3   Transit challenges

The study team identified several challenges to providing new transit service for the WMNF, namely:

- **Permeable forest boundaries.** There are no entrance gates to the WMNF, and there are hundreds of public access points to the forest, including parking lots, trailheads, day use areas, and campgrounds. This configuration makes it difficult to enforce payment of visitor use fees, concentrate parking for privately owned vehicles, limit access of privately owned vehicles, or implement other transportation demand management strategies that support transit systems.

- **Dispersed visitation.** Aside from several roads and high use sites during peak visitation season, visitation tends to be spread out throughout the forest (see the previous bullet). Without introducing disincentivizing use of privately owned vehicles, there are few, if any, individual sites with concentrated demand sufficient to necessitate or support traditional fixed-route transit systems.

- **Long distances between major recreation sites.** The White Mountain Trail National Scenic Byway is over 100 miles in length, and the Kancamagus Highway alone take about an hour traverse, one way. Long distances translate to long wait times between buses and inconvenience to potential riders. Adding more buses could reduce wait times and improve convenience but would require additional fuel, drivers, and capital investment.

- **Few disincentives to driving.** During most times of the year, there is little congestion on the roads and ample parking at recreation sites. Payment of visitor use fees (considered a parking fee because the ticket must be displayed in parked cars) is inconsistently enforced, as is Illegal overflow parking. In fact, to access the hundreds of access points to the WMNF, privately owned automobiles are quite convenient for visitors.

- **Low usage and unavailability of regional transit connections.** Despite bus service from Boston to towns near the WMNF, there are few regional transit connections to points within New England. Visitors are likely to arrive via privately owned vehicle, and they are apt to use their cars to access recreation opportunities within the forest.

- **Revenue challenges.** The persistence of any of the above challenges to a transit system suggests one of the two following outcomes: either transit ridership would be low, or a large number of buses would be needed to provide convenient service frequency over a large geography. Either way, providing a financially sustainable service would likely require user fees in excess of what visitors currently pay to access the WMNF by private automobile.

The above challenges to implementing transit to and within the WMNF are not insurmountable, as evidenced by the popularity and financial stability of AMC's Hiker Shuttle. Uncertain fuel prices and changing patterns related to outdoor recreation and car-ownership may also increase the demand by forest visitors for transit options. While significant expansion of transit in the forest may be challenging today, addressing current service gaps and beginning to consider transit options are key components of *5 Alternative transportation issues and options* and *6 Transportation scenarios*.

4.6   Bicycle infrastructure

The study team reviewed existing bicycle related data and existing or planned bicycle infrastructure within and surrounding the WMNF.

4.6.1   Bicycle accident and use data

The NHDOT maintains pedestrian and bicycle accident data. NHDOT data from Carroll, Coos, and Grafton counties during the period 2004-2007 indicate that the majority of bicycle accidents occur in the more developed urban areas, at relatively low speeds, with associated injuries. No cyclist fatalities were reported during this time. Trail use counts for cyclists are not maintained by the NHDOT or the WMNF.

4.6.2   New Hampshire Statewide Bicycle and Pedestrian Plan

The goal of the New Hampshire Statewide Bicycle and Pedestrian Plan (2000) is to "recognize, support and encourage bicycling and walking as alternatives to motorized forms of transportation."[8] The New Hampshire DOT has adopted this plan as the regional master planning document for the identification and implementation of the Statewide Bicycle Route System. The NHDOT recognizes that the "system is not universally ideal for bicyclists and pedestrians and improvements have to be made."[9] The plan outlines planning and design considerations, development, funding, and implementation of pedestrian

---

[8] New Hampshire Bicycle and Pedestrian Plan. 2000. P. 2 http://www.nh.gov/dot/programs/bikeped/documents/BikePedPlan.pdf
[9] *Ibid.*

and bicycle projects. The plan does not include anything specific to the WMNF. According to the NHDOT, the plan is scheduled for an update within the next two years.[10]

4.6.3   Existing infrastructure

The NH Statewide Bicycle and Pedestrian Plan establishes bicycle routes based on population size, proximity to recreational areas and services, and availability of existing roadway shoulders.[11] There are numerous NHDOT recommended paved bicycle routes through the WMNF which are included in the NH Statewide Bicycle Route System.[12] In most cases, these designated bicycle routes do not have accompanying road markings, like bicycle symbols, or bicycle lane markings.[13] In general, designated bicycles route have no requirements other than optional bicycle route signage.

Three designated recreational bicycle loops run entirely, or in part, through the WMNF. These routes include the following:

- Loop 201, a 44-mile route starting in Orford (outside the WMNF) that traverses NH 25/25A/10;
- Loop 202, a 40-mile route starting in Woodstock and featuring Franconia Bicycle Path, Franconia Notch State Park, the Robert Frost Museum, and Kinsman Notch that traverses US 3, NH 18, NH 116, SR/NH 112 (Kancamagus Highway); and
- Loop 203, a 36-mile route starting in Conway featuring Conway Village, Bear Notch Road, and the Bartlett covered bridge, that traverses Pasaconaway Rd, SR 112 (Kancamagus Highway), Bear Notch Rd., US 302, and West Side Rd.

Each of the designated loops provides opportunities for visitor access to recreational areas and the scenic views in the WMNF. Figure 29 illustrates these NHDOT White Mountain region designated bicycle routes. Figure 30, Figure 31, and Figure 32 provide a photo sampling of these on-road routes through the WMNF.

---

[10] Interview with NHDOT. September 2010.
[11] *Ibid.*
[12] NH Bike/Ped. White Mountain Region Bicycle Routes. Accessed December 15, 2010.
http://www.nh.gov/dot/programs/bikeped/maps/documents/wm_map.pdf.
[13] However, according to the NH DOT Statewide Bicycle and Pedestrian Plan (2000) a handful of projects for shared road bicycle lanes, and off roads paths identified in the original 1977 plan were built including, a bicycle path along NH Route 49 in the center of Waterville Valley. The bicycle loops discussed above remain on the statewide plan for bicycle routes in the WMNF Region. For more information see:
http://www.nh.gov/dot/programs/bikeped/documents/BikePedPlan.pdf.

Figure 29 - NHDOT White Mountain Region Bicycle Routes. Source: NHDOT

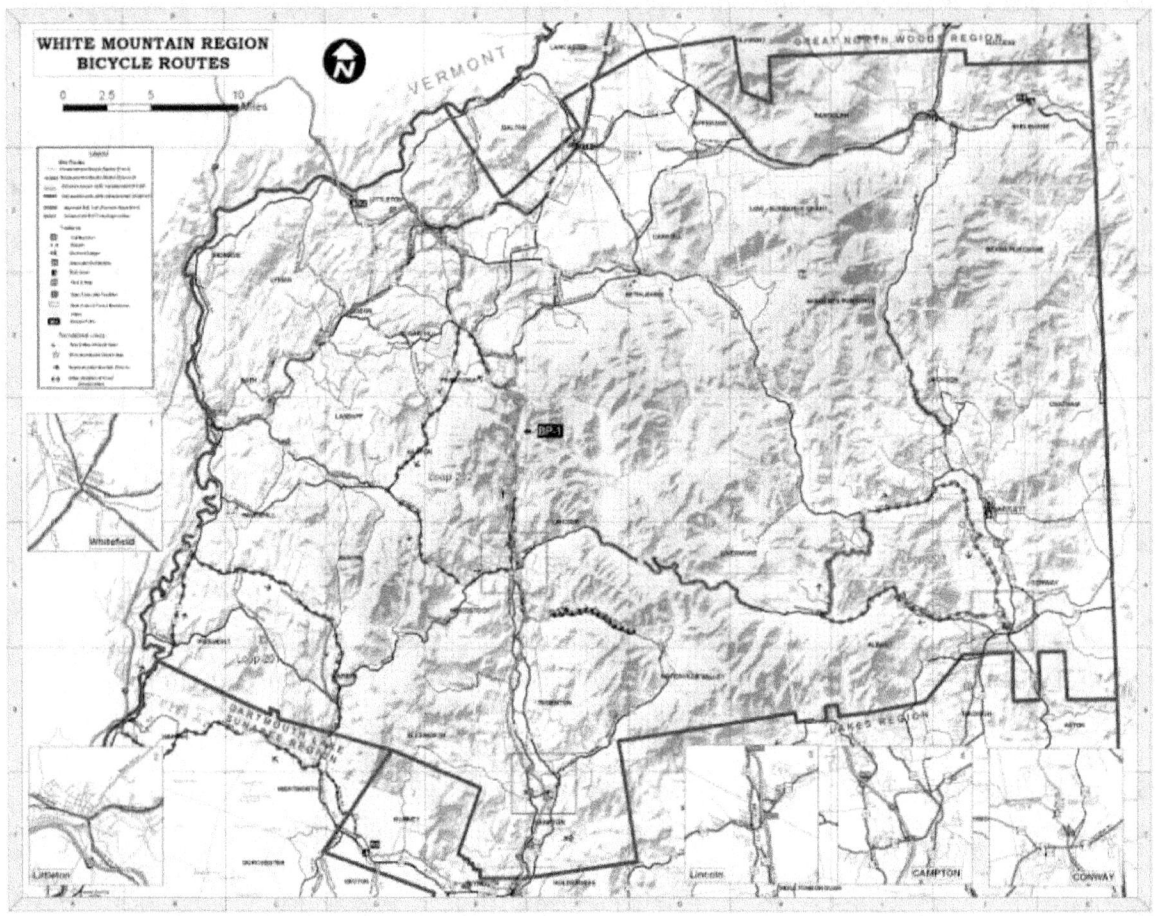

Figure 30 - Bicycle Loop 202 – Route 3 approaching Franconia Notch State Park. Source: Google Maps, 2009

Figure 31 - Bicycle Loop 202 – Route 116 towards Easton. Source: Google Maps, 2009

Figure 32 - Bicycle Loop 203 – Route 112 Kancamagus Highway approaching Bear Notch Road. Source: Google Maps, 2009

In addition, there are numerous off-road mountain biking trails throughout the WMNF. The WMNF website provides rules, recommendations, and general purpose trail maps for mountain biking on forest service roads. Mountain biking is relatively unrestricted throughout the WMNF. The WMNF does not maintain any paved off-road multi-use pathways for cycling. The New England Mountain Bike Association is responsible for trail maintenance on designated WMNF trails, and there are several bike shops in the area that cater to visitors. Locally published mountain bike trail maps show USFS-designated unpaved trails in the WMNF.

The gateway towns Lincoln and Twin Mountain have constructed off-road multi-use paths for cycling, walking, and other active transportation options.

Several sites within the WMNF are accessible from nearby towns or lodging areas by bicycle, providing car-free access opportunities. For example, sites within WMNF, like Lincoln Woods and Hancock Campground, are roughly four miles from the center of the Town of Lincoln and the major lodging areas at Loon Mountain Resort. Additionally, advanced, long-distance bicycle touring on the Kancamagus Highway and other roads throughout the WMNF, especially during peak foliage season, is becoming an increasingly popular activity.

There are currently no bicycle storage racks at WMNF recreation sites.

4.6.4 Planned bicycle infrastructure

There are several potential projects for extending existing bicycle paths or constructing new off-road bicycle and pedestrian paths between major lodging areas and recreational areas in the WMNF. Four potential bicycle path alignments include:

- A north-south extension of the existing Franconia Notch bicycle path to the Town of Lincoln;
- A bicycle path between Twin Mountain and Skookumchuck trailhead;
- A bicycle path between Twin Mountain and Bretton Woods; and
- A bicycle path between Bretton Woods and AMC Highland Center at Crawford Notch.

These potential projects are included in *6.4 Scenario 3 - Bicycle and pedestrian infrastructure*, and they can improve non-motorized access to visitor destinations throughout the WMNF.

4.7 Pre-trip traveler information

Pre-trip traveler information provides critical information to prospective travelers to help facilitate decisions about route choice, departure time, trip time, parking availability, and multi-modal transportation options. The study team conducted an inventory of existing pre-trip traveler information resources in the WMNF area and created a pilot website that attempts to include all alternative transportation traveler information for the region.

4.7.1 Traveler information inventory

The following are online traveler information resources for the region:

- **WMNF website.** The WMNF website has limited traveler information on its website. The "Contact Us" portion of the site provides addresses and directions to the WMNF offices and visitor information centers. The "Current Conditions" portion of the website lists travel warnings or notices regarding washed out bridges or roads. The "Law Enforcement and Investigations" portion of the site includes maps of motor vehicle use, National Forest System roads, National Forest System trails, and the areas on National Forest System lands in the WMNF that are designated for motor vehicle use. The "Recreational Activities" portion of the website has a section for "auto touring" which contains route suggestions for popular drives within and near the forest. The "Recreation Activities" portion of the website also includes guidance for road and mountain biking. For more information, see the website here: http://www.fs.fed.us/r9/forests/white_mountain/
- **White Mountains Attractions website.** The White Mountains Attractions Association is a non-profit membership organization that promotes numerous historic, cultural, recreational, and commercial destinations and services available in the White Mountains region. The website provides information on member amenities and includes maps, directions and mileage, seasonal travel tips and information on air transportation and ground transportation including, bus/shuttle, ferry, and rail options. For more information, see the website here: www.visitwhitemountains.com
- **NH DRED, Division of Travel and Tourism Development website.** The Division of Travel and Tourism Development promotes the New Hampshire visitor industry through coordinated

marketing opportunities, research and events. The website features a Planning and Travel Tools section that outlines air, train, bus, rental car traveler information, and provides maps and directions and domestic and international travel. For more information, see the website here: www.visitnh.gov

- **511nh.com.** The New Hampshire Department of Transportation provides the NH511 traveler information service to disseminate traffic data to commuters and travelers regarding weather-related road conditions, construction and congestion conditions on roadways. For more information, see the website here: www.nh.gov/dot/511
- **NHDOT Traveler/Commuter Information.** NHDOT provides links to traveler information resources throughout the state, including resources related to alerts, aviation, bicycle and pedestrians, road construction, maps, travel planning, public transportation, and weather. For more information, see the website here: http://www.nh.gov/dot/traveler/index.htm
- **Transportation provider information sources.** Individual transportation providers listed in *4.5.1 Transit inventory* each have resources of their own. Visit their individual website for more information.

In compiling this list of online traveler information resources, the study team learned there is no "one-stop shop" for all traveler information in the WMNF region. Instead, users have to visit multiple websites to learn about travel options, routes, schedules, maps, and anything else transportation-related. This decentralized approach to communicating information is an impediment to alternative transportation, particularly in an area like the WMNF where there are numerous disparate transit systems that do not intuitively connect together.

4.7.2 Alternative transportation pilot website

One approach to providing better traveler information in a region is to provide it all in one place. Cape Cod's Smart Guide provides a model for what can be done when regional stakeholders combine forces to create a single source of information.[14] As part of this study effort, the study team developed a pilot alternative transportation website to provide comprehensive traveler information for local transit, cycling, and rideshare options. The website, a screenshot of which is shown in Figure 33, is currently hosted by AMC. The website contains information on the following topics:

- Public transportation from Boston, MA and Concord, NH
- The AMC Hiker Shuttle
- Local transportation services
- Ride-sharing options
- Bicycling Resources

---

[14] For more information, visit http://www.smartguide.org/

Figure 33 - WMNF alternative transportation pilot website. Source: http://www.outdoors.org/conservation/transportation/

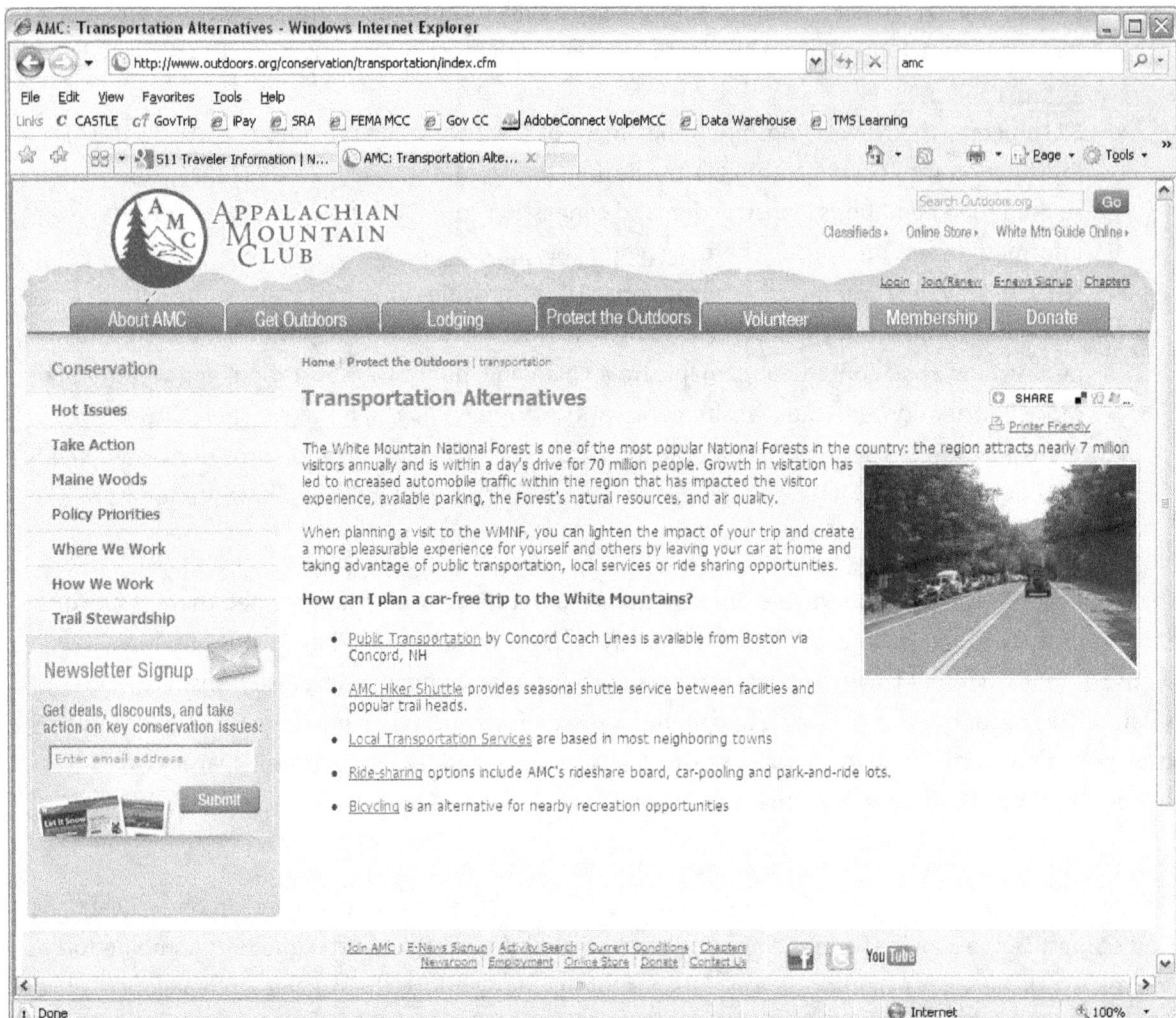

In planning and developing the alternative transportation pilot website, the study team learned valuable lessons that may direct future iterations of the site. Choosing an organization for hosting, creating, and maintaining the website required careful consideration. The location/affiliation of a traveler information resource would affect who might or might not find the resource. The WMNF website may be a logical location to store information related to the WMNF, but the WMNF was concerned that it could not host routes and schedules from private transportation providers on its website. The WMNF does not have the necessary resources to build and maintain a website itself. Maintenance of a traveler information resource, especially one with so many individual sources of information, is a critical task. One of the worst outcomes of a traveler information resource would be to provide incorrect or out of date information to travelers. Doing so could result in frustrating or unsafe travel experiences for visitors. Hosting the site on the AMC website, however, may restrict the potential audience to AMC members or non-members who "stumble" on the website. Where to host a site and how to maintain it are two questions that must be answered when creating a traveler information tool. Solutions to these challenges are presented in *6.3 Scenario 2 - Improved traveler information*.

4.8 WMNF recreational infrastructure analysis

The study team conducted an analysis of the recreational infrastructure and connections in the WMNF through field observations and geographic information systems (GIS) analysis. The objectives of the analysis were as follows:

- To seek opportunities to reduce vehicle traffic among WMNF sites;
- To reduce parking congestion;
- To increase access to recreational opportunities; and
- To create logical nodes around which to concentrate potential future transportation services.

The study considered 380 trailheads and activity sites, including parking areas, day use areas, trailheads, and campgrounds. Of these, approximately 50, shown in Figure 34, were identified as high-use or potential high-use sites based on assessment of two USFS/WMNF documents and experiential analysis. The first document included visitation stats for selected trailheads during limited timeframes. The second document included a list of trails with use ratings of Very High, High, Medium, or Low. Similar information was not available for parking areas, day use areas, trailheads, and campgrounds.

Experiential assessment (provided by AMC) was based on 15 years of familiarity with the WMNF gained by building GIS databases for Forest Service mapping work, hiking every trail on the WMNF, obtaining feedback from trail and hut crews that work on the Forest, and making observations from having lived, commuted, and recreated throughout this region.

Figure 34 - WMNF high-use recreation sites. Source: AMC

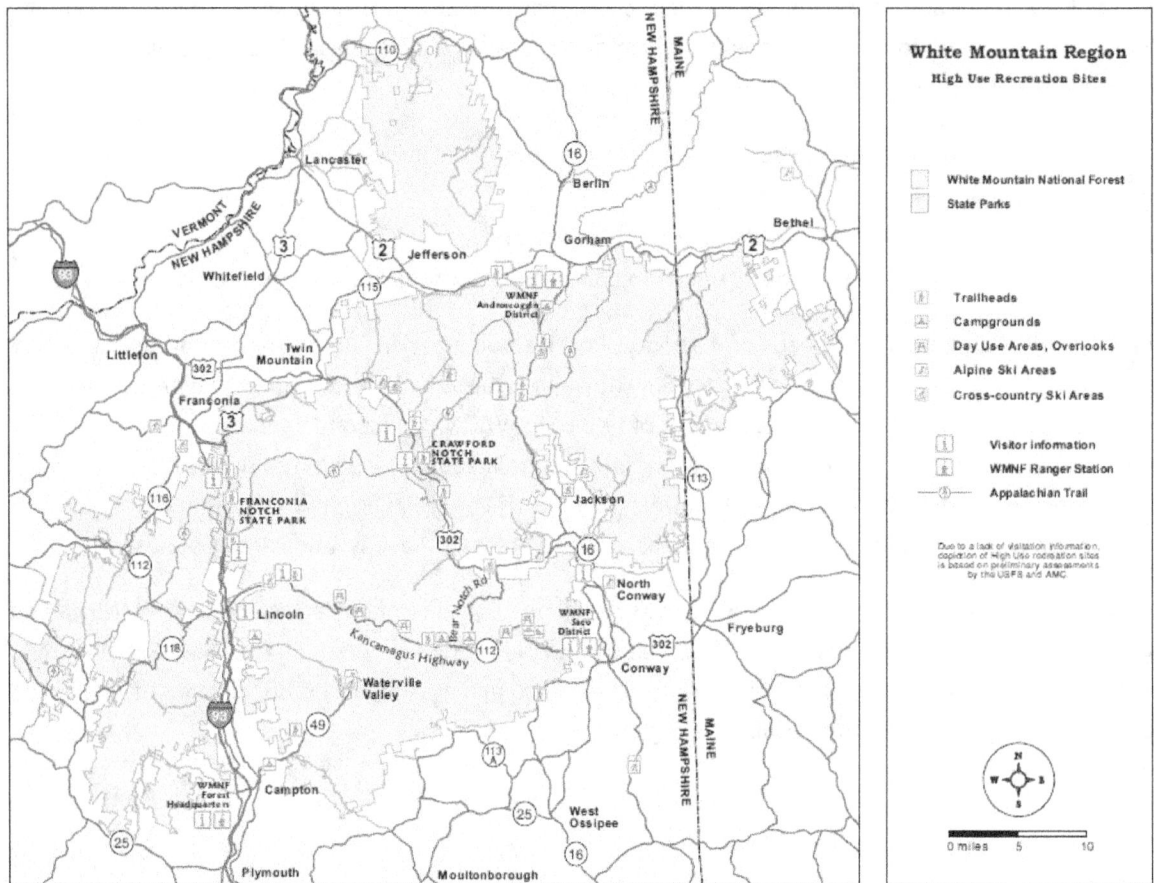

Locations of the high use sites may be used to identify potential transit stops. For example, a map of high use trailheads is shown in Figure 35 in relation to the existing AMC Hiker Shuttle route. All but a dozen high and very-high use trailheads are located along the primary highways, Kancamagus Highway / Route 112, Crawford Notch / Route 302, and Pinkham Notch / Route 16. These trailheads identify potential areas of expansion for the AMC Hiker Shuttle given its current primary business model, to provide transportation among AMC huts and trailheads. Future shuttle systems operating under other business models might examine day use areas, campgrounds, and parking areas, in addition to trailheads. This analysis shows that these high use areas are distributed throughout the existing road network in and around the WMNF.

Figure 35 - WMNF high-use trailheads near the existing AMC Hiker Shuttle route. Source: AMC

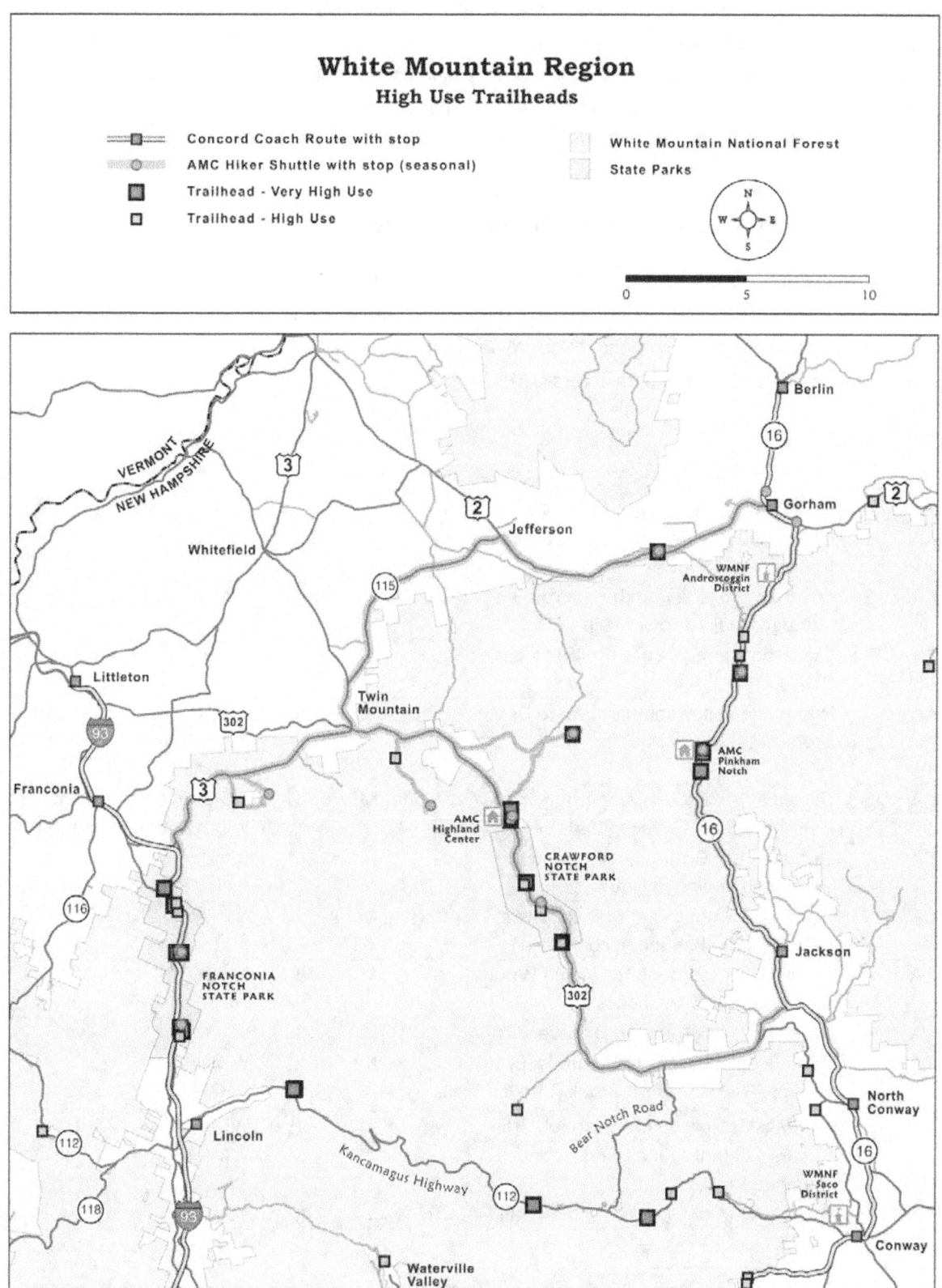

In addition to identifying high use sites, the study team identified 26 possible alternative transportation infrastructure projects that seek to reduce vehicle traffic among WMNF sites, reduce parking congestion, and increase non-motorized access to recreational opportunities. Table 3 summarizes these projects, including a description, use level, cost range, and partnership opportunities.[15] This inventory does not consider the current multi-purpose recreation bicycle paths in the area Lincoln-Loon, Presidential Range Rail Trail, and Franconia Notch Recreational Trail.

Infrastructure improvements considered access at a specific destination, and motorized and non-motorized connections to destinations. The improvements categories include:

- Provide non-motorized access from campgrounds to trailheads and day use areas access (CA);
- Provide non-motorized access from day use areas to trailheads (DA);
- Relocate trailheads to consolidate or provide parking (RT); and
- Build new trail and bike path access (TR).

Table 3 - WMNF possible alternative transportation infrastructure projects.

Type	ID	Description	Use Level	Cost Level	Partnership Opportunity
CA	1	Covered Bridge Campground (Passaconaway) to Boulder Loop Trail	H	L	WMNF
CA	2	Covered Bridge & Blackberry Crossing Campgrounds to Lower Falls DUA	M	M	WMNF
CA	3	Campton Campgrounds (Rt 49) to The Eddy DUA	M	H	NH DOT right of way
CA	4	Waterville Valley Campground to Drakes Brook & Sandwich Mtn Tr	L	M	NH DOT; Waterville Valley Athletic Improvement Association
CA	5	Osceola Vista Group Campground to Livermore Rd & Greeley Ponds Tr	M	M	Waterville Valley Athletic Improvement Assoc
CA	6	Osceola Vista Group Campground to Mt Tecumseh Trailhead (south)	M	M	Booth Creek/Waterville Valley Resort
CA	7	Dry River Campground to Frankenstein Cliff Tr (re-establish abandoned connector)	M	L	NH DRED, NH DOT
CA	8	Hancock Campground to Lincoln Woods Visitor Center & trailheads	M	L	NH DOT
CA	9	Big Rock Campground to Discovery Trail	H	L	WMNF
CA	10	Basin & Cold River Campgrounds (Evans) to Brickett Place, Bickford Brook & Royce Trails	M	M	WMNF
CA	11	Hastings Campground to Caribou Trail	L	H	WMNF
CA	12	Hastings Campground to Roost and Highwater trails	M	M	WMNF
DA	13	Dugway DUA to Moat Mountain Trail (south)	L	L	WMNF

---

[15] For the column entitled 'Partnership Opportunity', the designation 'WMNF' indicates proposed improvements that are entirely on WMNF land. Other entries indicate those agencies could partner in developing the improvement in conjunction with the WMNF.

Type	ID	Description	Use Level	Cost Level	Partnership Opportunity
RT	14	Relocate Mt Tecumseh TH (north) with East Pond TH (south) parking on Tripoli Rd	L	M	WMNF
RT	15	Relocate East Pond TH (north) with Otter Rocks Rest Area (Kanc)	L	M	WMNF
RT	16	Relocate Mt Tremont trailhead to Sawyer Rock Picnic Area (Rt 302)	L	M	WMNF
RT	17	Relocate Mt Meader trailhead to Cold River CG/DUA	L	M	WMNF
RT	18	Relocate Roost (south) trailhead to Wheeler Brook Road (provide parking)	L	M	WMNF
TR	19	Improve Lower Falls snowmobile trail from Zealand parking east to Bretton Woods	M	H	NH Bureau of Trails, NH DOT, Bretton Woods
TR	20	Improve XC ski trail(s) as bikepath from Bretton Woods to AMC Highland Ctr	L	H	AMC, Bretton Woods
TR	21	Build a recreation trail between the Pemi & CL Graham overlooks on the Kanc (HOL)	M	H	WMNF
TR	22	Build a multi-use recreational trail connecting PNVC, Wildcat, GGTOC in Pinkham Notch	M	H	NH DOT, AMC, Wildcat, GGTOC
TR	23	Integrate planned Twin Mountain Bicycle Path with Beaver Brook DUA & Twin Mtn	M	L	Carroll, lodging along Rt 3 in Twin Mtn
TR	24	Build a multi-use Bicycle Path from Lincoln to Franconia Notch/Flume	M	H	NH DOT, Town of Lincoln, NH DRED
TR	25	Extend Lincoln bike path from Loon Mtn to Lincoln Woods VC	M	H	NH DOT, Town of Lincoln, Loon Mtn
TR	26	Provide multi-use rec path from North Conway to Diana's Baths	M	H	Conway

The infrastructure analysis suggests possibilities to improve access among thirteen high use sites, relocate trailheads to consolidate parking demand at five sites, and build or extend bicycle paths and access trails at eight sites. Summarized another way, as shown in Table 4, the projects may be compared with one another in terms of estimated use and cost. Those projects with high use and low cost, such as 1 - Covered Bridge Campground (Passaconaway) to Boulder Loop Trail and 9 - Big Rock Campground to Discovery Trail might be examined first, while those projects with low use and high cost, 11 - Hastings Campground to Caribou Trail and 20 - Improve cross-country ski trail(s) as bikepath(s) from Bretton Woods to AMC Highland Center, might be considered last. Similarly, those with medium use intensity and low costs may be examined prior to those with medium use intensity and medium or high costs.

Table 4 - Use/cost analysis of possible alternative transportation infrastructure projects.

Use \ Cost	Low	Med	High
Low	13	4 7 14 15 16 17 18	11 20
Med	8 23	2 5 6 10 12	3 19 21 22 24 25 26
High	1 9		

All possible alternative transportation infrastructure projects would require extensive consideration by the Forest Service as well as NEPA compliance prior to design and implementation.

Information from this analysis compliments visitor characteristic and use data outlined in *4.1 Visitor group types* by providing information on specific sites that are both popular with WMNF visitors and also important to the planning of potential alternative transportation solutions in the WMNF.

4.9   Summary of existing conditions

This section described the existing transportation conditions in the White Mountains region including types of user groups and their travel needs and behaviors; results from several surveys regarding the transportation preferences of WMNF visitors; results of outreach activities related to transportation preferences; area transit systems and transit gaps; traffic counter data and locations for additional permanent counters; existing and planned bicycle infrastructure; pre-trip traveler information resources; and WMNF infrastructure that may support transit and infrastructure improvements that may reduce traffic and parking congestion. These findings from this section are summarized as follows:

- There are three distinct types of user groups that may benefit from alternative transportation in and around the WMNF: backcountry visitors; front-country visitors; and tourists and sightseers. These visitors have distinct needs, and improvements to alternative transportation should target one or more user groups. A fourth user group of roads in the region, through travelers, is not expected to benefit from alternative transportation to recreational destinations.
- The WMNF Visitor Use Monitoring Survey conducted in 2010 found the following:
  - There is potential demand for alternative transportation, not only in and around the WMNF, but also connecting to towns and cities in New England.

- Convenient alternative transportation that contributes to relaxing visits may be successful among some visitors, but some visitors may resist alternative transportation in favor of driving for pleasure.
  - There may be significant opportunities to work with the service sector, particularly hotels, when implementing ATS and visitor communications strategies.
  - Visitors place a high importance on traveler information and wayfinding, and any alternative transportation improvements should include these components.
- Three AMC surveys conducted in 2010 found the following:
  - Alternative transportation system improvements must be cost-competitive compared with driving (for users) and convenient to users as well.
  - Alternative transportation system improvements must be frequent and dependable.
  - Visitors to WMNF, and backcountry visitors with lots of gear in particular, may be willing to pay for hop-on-hop-off transit service. Willingness to pay for one-way and/or single-leg trips is unknown.
  - Actively managing parking and enforcing illegal parking restrictions may incentivize visitors to take transit.
- Transportation strengths for the WMNF area include the following:
  - AMC Hiker Shuttle;
  - Interstate bus connections to WMNF;
  - Regional and local, fixed route transit systems;
  - Multi-use paths;
  - State bicycle program;
  - Potential partners and stakeholders;
  - State Transportation Enhancement (TE) funds ($6 million every two years); and
  - Transit in Parks (TRIP) program funds.
- The region's transportation weaknesses include:
  - Seasonal traffic and parking congestion;
  - Few incentives to discourage the use of cars;
  - No comprehensive, regional transit system;
  - Long distances between sites/attractions;
  - Potential unsafe conditions for cycling;
  - No central source of alternative transportation pre-trip traveler information; and
  - Inadequate en-route signage and in wayfinding materials.
- Peak travel times in and around WMNF are as follows:
  - The months of July, August, and October;
  - Weekends, which on a daily basis account for more travel than weekdays, suggesting that recreational travel accounts for a significant portion of total travel in the area; and
  - Late weekend mornings through early afternoons.
- Permanent traffic counters should be installed in the following key corridors in the forest, specifically outside of developed areas which may generate a large proportion of local, non-recreational trips:

- o   Kancamagus Highway at Lincoln Woods Visitor Center;
- o   Kancamagus Highway at Dugway Road near Albany covered bridge;
- o   North of Jackson on Rt 16 at the Rocky Branch trailhead parking facility;
- o   South of Gorham on Rt 16 at Dolly Copp Road; and
- o   East of Carroll on Rt 302 at Mount Clinton Road.
- There exists a patchwork of existing transit systems near the WMNF. Besides the AMC Hiker Shuttle, none specifically serves visitors to WMNF.
- There exist gaps in service and schedule among the existing transit systems near the WMNF.
- The challenges to providing transit in and around the WMNF include:
  - o   Permeable forest boundaries;
  - o   Dispersed visitation;
  - o   Long distances between major recreation sites;
  - o   Few disincentives to driving;
  - o   Low usage and unavailability of regional transit connections; and
  - o   Revenue challenges.
- The majority of bicycle accidents occur in the more developed urban areas, at relatively low speeds, with associated injuries. No cyclist fatalities were reported during 2004-2007.
- The New Hampshire DOT has adopted the New Hampshire Statewide Bicycle and Pedestrian Plan as the master planning document for the identification and implementation of the Statewide Bicycle Route System. The plan does not include any findings or recommendations specific to the WMNF.
- Three designated recreational bicycle loops run entirely, or in part, through the WMNF:
  - o   Loop 201, a 44-mile route starting in Orford (outside the WMNF) that traverses NH 25/25A/10;
  - o   Loop 202, a 40-mile route starting in Woodstock and featuring Franconia Bicycle Path, Franconia Notch State Park, the Robert Frost Museum, and Kinsman Notch that traverses US 3, NH 18, NH 116, SR/NH 112 (Kancamagus Highway); and
  - o   Loop 203, a 36-mile route starting in Conway featuring Conway Village, Bear Notch Road, and the Bartlett covered bridge, that traverses Pasaconaway Rd, SR 112 (Kancamagus Highway), Bear Notch Rd., US 302, and West Side Rd.
- There are four potential bike path projects in and around the WMNF:
  - o   A north-south extension of the existing Franconia Notch bicycle path to the Town of Lincoln;
  - o   A bicycle path between Twin Mountain and Skookumchuck trailhead;
  - o   A bicycle path between Twin Mountain and Bretton Woods; and
  - o   A bicycle path between Bretton Woods and AMC Highland Center at Crawford Notch.
- There is no single source of online traveler information for the WMNF region. The study team created a pilot website which is hosted on the AMC website. Any new source of information must be located in a place easy for visitors to find and must be updated continuously to reflect changes to transportation providers' schedules.

- Recreational infrastructure analysis identified parking areas, day use areas, trailheads, and campgrounds throughout the road network in and around the WMNF as potential transit nodes and stops.
- In addition to identifying transit opportunities, recreational infrastructure analysis identified possibilities to improve non-motorized access among thirteen high use sites, relocate trailheads to consolidate parking demand at five sites, and build or extend bicycle paths and access trails at eight sites.

The findings from the existing conditions informed creation of the issues and options in *5 Alternative transportation issues and options* and the scenarios in *6 Transportation scenarios*.

5 Alternative transportation issues and options

Based on the review of existing conditions, and discussed and confirmed during outreach activities, the study team created sets of alternative transportation issues and alternative transportation options. Issues encompass specific problems or challenges related to alternative transportation. Options represent potential solutions to one or more issues. Both the transportation issues and options relate back to the goals of the study by seeking to improve car-free travel options and identifying options for additional alternative transportation planning or implementation projects.

Transportation issues and options are grouped into the following four transportation categories (previously defined in Table 1):

- Traveler information/wayfinding/signage (TI);
- Bicycle and pedestrian (BP);
- Transit (TR); and
- Policy and planning (PP).

5.1 Alternative transportation issues

The study team identified issues relating to alternative transportation in and around the WMNF through review and analysis of existing conditions and through input and feedback from stakeholder outreach activities described above in *4.3 Stakeholder outreach*. The transportation issues generally encompass the following topics:

- Identified transportation-related problems in the WMNF region.
- Opportunities to improve the physical environment to support alternative transportation initiatives.
- Changes to WMNF resource management policies as they impact transportation issues in the forest.

Table 5 provides the set of WMNF alternative transportation issues identified by the study team and verified by stakeholders at the stakeholder workshop described in *4.3 Stakeholder outreach*.

Table 5 - WMNF alternative transportation issues.

Issue ID	Issue desription
TI_01	Opportunity to improve en route wayfinding roadway/wayside signage in and around the WMNF (e.g. seasonal road closures and unimproved roads for winter travelers, information on popular destinations, etc.).
TI_02	Opportunity to improve pre-trip communication of regional/local transportation options to the public and tourists (e.g. information about local towns and regional bicycling opportunities, how to park and use transit/bicycle during an extended visit, etc.).
BP_01	Lack of adequate bicycle/pedestrian infrastructure (e.g. crosswalks, designated bicycle parking, wayfinding signage, information, concessions, and secured lockers) at recreational destinations throughout the WMNF.
BP_02	Opportunities to improve accommodation (e.g. adding crosswalks, bicycle lanes, signage, etc.) for bicycles/pedestrians on roads to and through the WMNF.

Issue ID		Issue desription
BP_03		Potential for road user conflicts/safety concerns among different road user types, (e.g. pedestrian, cyclists, automobiles).
TR_01	SERVICE GAPS	No east-west transit service between Lincoln and Conway along Route 112 / Kancamagus Highway.
TR_02		Lack of local transit service to recreational destinations, including Franconia Notch State Park.
TR_03		No transit service that connects Concord Coach Lines in Plymouth with Waterville Valley.
TR_04		Lack of inter-state transit service from Maine, Vermont, or the NH seacoast (I-95 corridor).
TR_05	COORDINATION GAPS	Lack of coordinated scheduled stops between the AMC Hiker Shuttle and the Gorham Trolley.
TR_06		Lack of coordinated schedule/transit transfers in Littleton between Tri-Town and Concord Coach Lines.
TR_07		Lack of coordinated schedule/transit transfers in Pinkham Notch between AMC Hiker Shuttle and Concord Coach Lines.
PP_01		Opportunities for improved coordination among WMNF staff, North Country Council, and North Country Transit or other transportation providers/initiatives.
PP_02		Need for champion leader/council for alternative transportation initiatives.
PP_03		Gaps in transportation related management data that is required for ATS planning efforts (e.g. year round vehicle counts in the WMNF to expose seasonal increases in visitation, parking lot use, origin and destination information of visitors, etc.)
PP_04		Automobile congestion on the Kancamagus and other roads during peak visitation.
PP_05		Unauthorized parking on roadway shoulders resulting from Full parking lots or lack of authorized parking in some areas.
PP_06		Opportunities to better communicate to the public the growing number of discrete transportation initiatives (e.g. Coordinated transit/human service transportation plan, regional plans; park and ride, Carroll County transit, and transportation planning at WMNF).

5.2 Alternative transportation options

The study team developed an initial set of transportation options based on the issues identified in *5.1 Alternative transportation issues*. The study team sought feedback on these at the Alternative Transportation Stakeholder Workshop. The options represent potential planning and implementation actions that the WMNF and its partners can take to improve alternative transportation services in the WMNF region. Based on feedback from the workshop, the study team refined and amended these options. Several options, shown in Table 6, included in the initial lists were removed because they failed to directly promote alternative transportation or diverged from the scope of the study.

Table 6 - WMNF alternative transportation options removed from consideration.

Option category	Option description
TI	Develop an audio/video tour for visitors to WMNF and its surrounding communities.
TR	Provide a central dispatch for on-demand services.
PP	Expand parking lots that are habitually overcrowded.
PP	Provide pull-in (off road) parking at trailheads where parking is currently on shoulder.

Table 7 lists the final alternative transportation options. The study team and the stakeholders acknowledge additional planning and review beyond the scope of this study would be necessary to realize any of the options presented in Table 7. Additional planning activities would include the following:

- **Route or site-specific analysis of transit, bicycle, and pedestrian infrastructure.** The addition of transit service routes and stops, bicycle lanes, off-road multi-use path paths, pedestrian crossings, locations of wayfinding signs, and other ATS infrastructure needs to be considered against several factors, including current and projected traffic volumes, level of service of the road segments or intersections, crash data analysis from NH DOT data, current sign locations, identification of new sign locations, roadway safety audit of areas targeted for specific interventions, and jurisdictional issues.

- **Transit service plan formulations.** In the case of extending, or creating a new transit service, a detailed transit service plan would be required. Such a plan would determine the demand for transit and the appropriate scale of a system, its composition, and operations. It would define transit system requirements, system operations, route alternatives, and provide final recommendations, including a funding and operations plan. Transit system requirements include information on parking locations, fee collection, transit shelters, vehicle storage and maintenance facilities, fueling options, and transit fleet characteristics. Transit system operations include information about potential partnerships, operation seasons, times of operation, acceptable vehicle headways (the time between shuttles, which indicate how long visitors wait), vehicle ownership, and operations. Transit route alternatives would consider varying route alternatives and the associated operational costs of each option.

- **Lifecycle costs estimates.** Capital, operations, and maintenance costs are not currently identified for individual options. For example, the costs of bicycle racks, or the per-mile construction costs of multi-use paths, bicycle lane striping, or the number of wayfinding specific signs are not provided, and would have to be identified prior to selecting options for implementation.

- **Asset management plans.** Long-term asset management plans to guide decision making for the Forest Service or other entities are not identified. Such plans would inventory existing infrastructure or owned assets, create maintenance or replacement schedules, and annual asset conditions assessment, and identify trends in assets types (e.g. age, relevance) to inform lifecycle planning.[16]

Table 7 - WMNF alternative transportation options.

Option ID	Option description	
TI_01	Develop and market a web-based travel information resource to and through WMNF that includes car-free travel information and place-based traveler information in relation to local recreational opportunities.	
TI_02	Implement a "travel trainer" program to educate travel, tourism, and recreation partners (e.g. member of White Mountain Attractions, resorts/hotels, business owners, etc.) about alternative travel opportunities in and around WMNF.	
TI_03	Provide local establishments with information about car-free recreation opportunities.	
TI_04	Identify and work to implement roadway signage in specific problem areas (e.g. Bear Notch Road seasonal road closure information).	
BP_01	Improve bicycling/pedestrian infrastructure (e.g. crosswalks, designated bicycle parking, wayfinding signage, information, concessions, and secured lockers) at recreational sites in the WMNF (e.g. Day Use areas/campgrounds, trailheads) and at major lodging access nodes (e.g. surrounding towns/areas, resorts, etc.).	
BP_02	Improve non-motorized access (e.g. extend existing, or construct new on-road and off-road, paved and non-paved trails) between recreational sites in the WMNF (e.g. Day Use areas/campgrounds) and at major lodging access nodes (e.g. surrounding towns/areas, resorts, etc.).	
BP_03	Extend the Franconia Recreation Bike Path to the Town of Lincoln.	
BP_04	Construct a bicycle path between Twin Mountain and Skookumchuck trailhead.	
BP_05	Construct a bicycle path between Twin Mountain and Bretton Woods.	
BP_06	Relocate trailheads to consolidate access points.	
BP_07	Add crosswalks in high pedestrian/bicycle travel areas.	
TR_01		Develop a tour/shuttle route on the Kancamagus Highway during peak visitation.
TR_02		Develop a transit service from Lincoln to the Franconia State Park area to connect with the Franconia bike path.
TR_03	SERVICE GAPS	Extend AMC hiker shuttle, to Conway / North Conway / Lincoln or to other hubs / nodes.
TR_04		Develop a transit/shuttle/bicycle trailer service to popular bicycle loops.
TR_05		Provide direct connections with NCT and Carroll County Transit system.
TR_06		Develop bus service on Route 16 from Dover to North Conway to serve travelers from the south traveling to the WMNF.
TR_12		Develop transit service from Littleton into the WMNF.
TR_07		Develop a regional transit service from Campton at I-93 exit 28 to connect Waterville Valley and Plymouth.

---

[16] Department of the Interior Guidance and Structure for Bureau Asset Management Plans. Accessed February 2, 2011. http://www.doi.gov/pam/AMPTemplate092105.pdf

Option ID		Option description
TR_08		Develop a transportation hub / center for regional bus travelers located primary in Lincoln / Conway / N. Conway or secondary in Littleton / Gorham / Plymouth / Campton / Franconia / Twin Mountain.
TR_09		Develop an inter-state transit service to the WMNF (e.g. Portland, ME via Fryeburg, ME to connect with the Amtrak Downeaster, and Boston to ME bus systems / Central Maine via Bethel, ME and Gorham, NH / Portsmouth, NH via Dover (Rt 16 corridor) / Central Vermont via St. Johnsbury and Littleton, NH).
TR_10	COORDINATION GAPS	Designate and promote Park and Ride lots in the White Mountain region under the NH DOT Rideshare program.
TR_11		Promote scheduling coordination with regional and local public and private transportation providers (e.g. AMC Hiker Shuttle and Concord Coach Lines at Pinkham Notch Visitor Center).
PP_01		Create an Alternative Transportation Technical Advisory Committee for the WMNF region.
PP_02		Improve coordination with White Mountain Attractions and encourage WMA to host car-free traveler information.
PP_03		Improve coordination with DRED Division of Travel and Tourism Development to i) include more information about WMNF on the visitnh.gov website and ii) host car-free traveler information to the region.
PP_04		Improve coordination with North Country Council to expand transportation planning efforts in the region to consider needs of recreational visitors and car-free travel for recreational purposes.
PP_05		Work with the NHDOT to cite permanent traffic counters at designated locations throughout the WMNF.
PP_06		Improve parking resource and management (e.g. collect information on parking lot capacities, develop a method to track occupancy and use).
PP_07		Quantitatively identify high use recreational areas to aid in ATS planning efforts as a means to improve access management to trails and natural features.
PP_08		Explore opportunities for vehicle sharing with ski resorts that run winter shuttle systems.
PP_09		Conduct roadway safety audit to investigate widening road shoulders for cyclists, reducing speed limits, improving pedestrian crossings, and identifying pavement repairs.
PP_10		Expand, and enforce recreational fee structure and explore as a means to fund ATS within WMNF.
PP_11		Explore opportunities to partner with the North Country Scenic Byways Council on projects related to the White Mountains Trail and the Kancamagus Scenic Byway- and potentially other designated trails in the area.
PP_12		Improve tour bus management with private operators that visit WMNF (e.g. require Special Use Permits for tour vehicles, or include tour bus operators in the Forest Service's Outfitter Guide Program).
PP_13		Create a Friends Group to manage aspects of WMNF visitor experience.

Option ID	Option description
PP_14	Create a National Forest Interpreter Program and include an interpretive service on potential transit routes to increase the value of transit among visitors.
PP_15	Explore tolling opportunities on the Kancamagus Highway as a means to fund alternative transportation improvements at WMNF.
PP_16	Partner with business communities and chambers to substantiate transit options that serve commuters and workforce needs and recreation.
PP_17	Roadway safety audit to investigate widening road shoulders for cyclists, reducing speed limits, improving pedestrian crossings, and identifying pavement repairs.

At the Alternative Transportation Stakeholder Workshop, participants divided into four small groups and discussed the options in each alternative transportation category that they considered as candidates for further consideration. Each group had ten minutes to discuss the identified options, add options to the list, and agree on two options for primary consideration or implementation. Each of the following four sections summarizes the discussions that took place for each alternative transportation option category. Refer to Table 7 for the text of each option. This exercise helped to inform the development of the potential alternative transportation models described in the *6 Transportation scenarios*.

5.2.1 Traveler Information / wayfinding / signage options discussion

Across all four groups, the stakeholders were quick to organize the various options in terms of "active options" (those which require the visitor to seek out information, such as website, books, and brochures) and "passive options" (those which the visitor simply receives information, such as signs). The consensus was that active options for accessing traveler information would be preferred. Specifically, this was reflected in a desire to avoid additional roadside signage and the overall support for Option TI_01, an intuitive, regionally specific website that could be closely integrated with existing tourism resources.

There was a general sense of uncertainty regarding who would be responsible for the implementation and maintenance of any of the four presented options. Some stakeholders felt that implementation should be the sole responsibility of the USFS, while others felt that any implementation should emerge from multi-stakeholder partnerships created specifically for the purpose of promoting alternative transportation. In addition, there was uncertainty regarding the audience at which these options should be aimed. Some felt that locals and local recreationists should be the primary focus, while others felt that any work should be aimed at out-of-state tourists.

An additional option that was mentioned by each of the stakeholder groups was some sort of resource (most likely a downloadable application) for smart phones. A drawback to this idea, however, is the current inconsistency in cell service throughout the region, especially among the various service providers.

Option TI_02 (a travel-trainer program to educate visitors) was not well received by the four groups of stakeholders. They were uncertain that visitors to the area would be willing to receive education, and unclear as to who, specifically, would do the training. When prompted to consider volunteers or other regional "ambassadors," the response was generally positive but tempered with skepticism regarding the availability of actual volunteers and the ability of the USFS to adequately recruit, train, and retain a volunteer workforce for this program. Suggested modifications to this option included integrating the program with the existing 511 service, or somehow merging it into Option TI_01.

Option TI_01 (a web-based travel information resource) received the strongest support from the four stakeholder groups. The stakeholders emphasized three key points: i) that the web-based travel information resource must be integrated into an existing tourism resource (most likely visitnh.gov); ii) that there is opportunity to fold Options TI_01 and TI_03 into the web-based resource; and iii) that the inclusion of a significant marketing component is necessary to make visitors aware of any new alternative transportation resources.

An option that suggested an audio/video tour for visitors received the least amount of support from the four stakeholder groups. The relevance of this option to alternative transportation was unclear, and there was uncertainty as to whether or not visitors to the WMNF region would demand such a service. There was a sense that this option could be somehow combined with Option TI_01, although the stakeholders were not specific as to what this would look like.

Option TI_03 (provide local establishments with car-free information) was met with indifference. Some stakeholders questioned the incentive of local establishments to provide such information, while others saw this option as the main opportunity to reach out to locals regarding the importance and availability of alternative transportation throughout the WMNF region. Of the four options, there was a sense that this would be the easiest and least expensive to implement.

Overall, participants regarded Option TI _01 as a popular option.

5.2.2 Bicycle and pedestrian options discussion

In general, participants felt that improving the cycling and pedestrian environments in and around the WMNF are positive moves for the WMNF to consider. One WMNF staff person commented that the option to provide bicycle amenities like bicycle parking, secured lockers, or concessions at popular trailheads had never been considered by the Forest Service but could improve the situation for cyclists that want to ride to these locations. Concerns focused on the responsibility and feasibility of implementing the improvements. Some WMNF staff members were wary of installing new bicycle racks or constructing/extending and maintaining new bicycle paths given current resource shortfalls. Other concerns included the difficulty of engineering safe sidewalks and crosswalks in high through-traffic areas and the difficulty of constructing expanded roadway shoulders to improve on-road cycling where there may be right-of-way, environmental, or topography issues that increased costs significantly or precluded construction at all.

Several other participants expressed interest in creating regional bicycle connections, including the ability to bring bicycles aboard regional buses.[17] Other comments included working to improve existing bicycle and pedestrian infrastructure, for example, leveraging opportunities to connect the Franconia Recreational Bicycle Path to Lincoln. The need to improve on-line bicycling information so that people know the suitability of bicycling conditions on trails and routes (e.g. on-road, off-road, advanced, family friendly etc.); and how to get to the routes from major lodging areas (e.g. Lincoln, Conway, etc.). Lastly, participants suggested that bicycling and walking could be marketed by the NHDOT and others as benefiting private businesses. It was noted that the tourism business generated through cycling in many states is quite significant. The NHDOT provides an online map of designated bicycle loops, expanding upon that information in the ways mentioned above could help encourage recreational travel by bicycle, but also the legitimacy of cycling on roads in and around the WMNF.

Overall, participants regarded Option BP_01, Option BP_02, Option BP_03, Option BP_04, and Option BP_05 as popular options.

5.2.3 Transit options discussion

There were 13 transit options for the participants to consider. Some of these were specific to location (e.g., closing a particular service gap) while others were general or conceptual (promoting coordination), so it was challenging for participants to evaluate the relative merits. Participants were asked if there were any statistics or survey data that would substantiate an interest or public demand for any of the service-gap options. There were no suggestions

There was a very strong consensus for Option TR_08 (developing transportation hubs) and Option TR_10 (designating park-and-ride lots), with the ultimate vision of establishing a shuttle service along the Kancamagus Highway (NH Route 112) between inter-modal hubs in Lincoln and Conway. A common perception was that hubs and park-and-ride lots would have greater utility being combined than remaining separate. They could including visitor information services, amenities, concessions, a focal point that promotes awareness of public transportation, public safety (leaving a car unattended, possibly lighted at night), and an entry portal for visitors to the area. These facilities would serve as inter-regional, inter-modal transportation centers that would attract service providers, and afford travelers with a one-stop option for connections, transfers, and information. The list of potential towns or nodes for locating a hub would need to be screened for optimal use and economic benefit. Local Chambers of Commerce may well be interested in the opportunities for traveler services.

Comments more specific to Option TR_01 (a Kancamagus Shuttle) cited this as an obvious choice for a pilot program, noting that its viability would be greatly enhanced by operating from/to inter-modal hub facilities. Although the Kancamagus was named as a specific route, the designated White Mountain Trail Scenic Byway (including Routes 112, 3, 16, and the Bear Notch Road) was seen as the "core" area where transportation services should be focused. The various gaps between existing services should be evaluated for their connectivity to a corridor or inter-modal hub.

---

[17] Currently, bicycles are allowed on a first-come first-served basis on Concord Coach and C&J regional bus services, if there is room in the cargo hold. Bicycles aboard are not guaranteed.

Other transit options that received support were Option TR_11 (promoting scheduling coordination among service providers), and Option TR_03 (extending existing shuttle services to connect to hubs/nodes). These options represent opportunities for entrepreneurial operators on a local scale, compared to a scenario where one service is expected to serve a wide range of needs. Furthermore, coordinating and extending existing services could be achieved in the near term with lower capital investment requirements (upgrading services as compared to start-up). It was generally felt that there was no reason not to go for this "lower hanging fruit" while bigger projects were evaluated and planned.

Anecdotal comments referred to the Conway Scenic Railroad and the Route 16 rail corridor (existing and future, respectively) as transit options. There has also been some interest expressed for extending a potential Portland-to-Bethel ME passenger rail service to Gorham NH, a possible transportation hub for the White Mountains.

Overall, participants regarded TR_01, TR_08, TR_10, and TR_11 as popular options.

5.2.4 Policy and planning options discussion
Many groups had difficulty deciding on a priority policy or planning option to pursue. Much of the discussion focused on options that seemed to be similar, suggesting that some options could be combined. Discussion focused on means and methods to fund projects. There was no interest in categorically expanding parking facilities, or in providing pull-in parking from shoulders. Option PP_17 received positive feedback, and the suggestion that it should include wildlife collision avoidance as a component.

Participants voted option PP_16 as the highest overall voted priority. It was discussed that there would be great value to identifying a champion of alternative transportation planning in the White Mountains region, and developing partnerships for implementing long-term transportation projects or initiatives.

Participants were interested in a policy strategy for advertising / promoting ATS travel, in terms of specifically reducing vehicle miles traveled throughout the White Mountains region. In general the groups did not favor en route interpretation services.

Overall, participants regarded Option PP_01 and Options PP_11 through PP_16 as popular options.

6 Transportation scenarios

Based on the various information collected, analyzed, and researched during this study, and based on the discussion generated at the Alternative Transportation Stakeholder Workshop, the study team developed six transportation scenarios to inform future transportation planning possibilities for the WMNF. The transportation scenarios represent alternative transportation implementation or management visions in and around the White Mountains and draw from several of the four transportation categories as described in *3 Alternative transportation systems*.

Each transportation scenario is composed of a conceptual description, a discussion of the transportation issues it addresses, and how the scenario might be implemented. Following each scenario is a table of the options that comprise the scenario, followed by a table of options that are related to, though not included in the scenario.

In addition to the six scenarios, the study team identified a set of 'transportation management improvements' that represent planning and management activities the WMNF staff may pursue irrespective of the other options or scenarios. These activities relate to improving transportation related data collection, partnership building and coordination of existing transit services.

The scenarios and transportation management improvements aim to provide the WMNF and its partners a framework for continued discussions about alternative transportation planning in the White Mountains. The scenarios are not meant to be mutually exclusive, and the WMNF and its stakeholders may use the lists of issues and options presented earlier to develop new scenarios of their own.

The remainder of this section presents the transportation management improvements followed by six alternative transportation scenarios.

6.1 Transportation management improvements

The study team has identified transportation management improvements that could be first steps to improving alternative transportation in and around the WMNF. The options within this section, shown in Table 8, can be pursued in addition to any of the other options and/or scenarios described in this report. Options related to transportation management improvements are listed in Table 9.

6.1.1 Strengthen existing / build new relationships

As evidenced by the outreach activities conducted during this study, a number of stakeholders in the area have an interest in transportation. To further alternative transportation, the WMNF can acknowledge and pursue this common interest with regional stakeholders. While one option may be to create a regional alternative transportation advisory committee, another option may be for the Forest Service and its alternative transportation stakeholders to become active in the existing transportation planning activities in the region. Potential stakeholders and existing activities are as follows:

- **North Country Council** – The North Country Council Regional Transportation Plan recognizes the impacts of increased recreational travel demand in the region. The Forest Service may become active in regional transportation planning efforts by participating in planning meetings and representing the interests and needs of recreational travelers. In this way alternative transportation and the desire for car free recreational transportation could be introduced and eventually included in the regional transportation plan. The Forest Service could seek a permanent seat on the Transportation Advisory Council.

- **Regional Coordinating Council** – Part of New Hampshire Governor's Taskforce on Community Transportation effort to create statewide transportation infrastructure that is both affordable and accessible to the citizens of New Hampshire, the Grafton-Coos and Carroll County RCCs seeks to expand public transportation services and options, including volunteers, carpooling, taxi services, and rail, bicycle and pedestrian paths. The Forest Service and its stakeholders may work with or become part of these councils on planning activities and represent the unique needs of recreational travelers.
- **Transit operators** – The Forest Service may reach out to Tri-Cap and its constituent transit systems, the AMC shuttle, and Concord Coach Lines to close service gaps (see below).
- **White Mountain Attractions** – The Forest Service could address alternative transportation and coordination of tour groups in its ongoing relationship with White Mountain Attractions.
- **Local governments** – The Forest Service could have a presence at town planning meetings and hearings and seek opportunities to collaborate on alternative transportation projects. Towns often submit grant applications for transportation enhancement funds for bicycle and pedestrian projects.
- **Ski resorts** – The Forest may address alternative transportation in its relationships with nearby ski resorts.

Furthermore, because the WMNF commonly draws visitors from all over New England and is a major recreation and tourism destination within the state, the Forest Service may seek to strengthen relationships with state agencies such as NHDOT or the New Hampshire Department of Recreation and Economic Development's Division of Travel and Tourism. With the former, the Forest Service may seek to provide input in the development of the statewide transportation plan, in the planning and communications about park and ride lots, and bicycle route planning in and around the forest. With the latter, the Forest Service may seek opportunities to expand communications about car-free transportation to visitors and tourists.

6.1.2   Close existing transit service gaps

Car-free travel to and within the region could be improved by addressing spatial and temporal gaps among existing transportation services, as documented in *5.2 Alternative transportation options*. Closing these gaps would be compatible with any of the options and scenarios outlined in this study. The Forest Service, though not responsible for these services or their schedules, may take on the role of catalyst and work with the various service providers to synchronize routes and schedules. A seamless regional transit network will be a stronger foundation on which to build additional alternative transportation features and services.

6.1.3   Conduct additional and ongoing data collection

The WMNF may expand its data collection efforts in order to:

- Justify the need for alternative transportation in the region.

- Identify and prioritize individual projects for implementation.
- Create a qualitative baseline of existing transportation conditions.
- Monitor transportation conditions over time in response to project implementations.

Specific data collection improvements include:

- **Monitoring parking supply and demand** – The Forest Service could conduct an inventory of parking spaces throughout the Forest and use volunteer staff to monitor parking usage during peak periods. Monitoring parking supply and demand could help quantitatively identify and compare areas that experience parking overflows, identify and prioritize alternative transportation and parking projects, and analyze effectiveness of recreation fee collection by area.
- **Monitoring traffic flow** – The Forest Service could continue to work with NHDOT to install permanent traffic counters at designated locations throughout the WMNF, as described in *4.4.4 Key findings*. Traffic counters will allow Forest Service to quantitatively describe vehicle travel patterns in and around the forest and to help plan ATS to replace a portion of these car trips.
- **Monitoring usage of recreation areas** – The Forest Service could use volunteer staff to monitor use of day use areas, trailheads, campgrounds, and other recreation areas to quantitatively characterize those sites most visited and those sites which would most benefit from inclusion in an alternative transportation system.
- **Monitor tour bus activity and impacts** – The Forest Service could monitor the impacts of tour buses on congestion, parking, and access at popular recreation sites throughout the Forest. Verification of adverse impacts caused by tour buses and tour bus visitors may justify increased management tour bus activities and flow under the Forest's special use permitting program.

Table 8 - Options comprising the transportation management improvements.

Option ID	Option description
PP_02	Improve coordination with White Mountain Attractions and encourage WMA to host car-free traveler information.
PP_03	Improve coordination with DRED Division of Travel and Tourism Development to i) include more information about WMNF on the visitnh.gov website and ii) host car-free traveler information to the region.
PP_04	Improve coordination with North Country Council to expand transportation planning efforts in the region to consider needs of recreational visitors and car-free travel for recreational purposes.
PP_05	Work with the NHDOT to cite permanent traffic counters at designated locations throughout the WMNF.
PP_06	Improve parking resource and management (e.g. collect information on parking lot capacities, develop a method to track occupancy and use).
PP_07	Quantitatively identify high use recreational areas to aid in ATS planning efforts as a means to improve access management to trails and natural features.
PP_12	Improve tour bus management with private operators that visit WMNF (e.g. require Special Use Permits for tour vehicles, or include tour bus operators in the Forest Service's Outfitter Guide Program).
TR_10	Designate and promote Park and Ride lots in the White Mountain region under the NH DOT Rideshare program
TR_11	Promote scheduling coordination with regional and local public and private transportation providers.

Table 9 - Options related to the transportation management improvements.

Option ID	Option description
PP_01	Create an Alternative Transportation Technical Advisory Committee for the WMNF region.
PP_08	Explore opportunities for vehicle sharing with ski resorts that run winter shuttle systems.
PP_10	Expand and enforce recreational fee structure and explore as a means to fund ATS within WMNF.
TI_01	Develop and market a web-based travel information resource to and through WMNF that includes car-free travel information and place-based traveler information in relation to local recreational opportunities.

6.2 Scenario 1 - Alternative transportation technical advisory committee

This scenario describes the creation of a regional Alternative Transportation Technical Advisory Committee that works towards the following activities:

- Creating sustainable, mutually beneficial partnerships for sharing information;
- Identifying funding sources and procuring funding;
- Coordinating existing transportation services; and

- Marketing various transportation alternatives throughout the WMNF region.

Committee members could include stakeholders like WMNF staff, regional transportation and human service transportation providers, tourism groups, ski areas, state government, and regional planning staff. Entities with natural affiliations include the Regional Coordinating Council, North Country Transit, and the Transportation Advisory Committee at the North Country Council, the North Country Scenic Byways Council, and others. The work of the committee would build upon the products of this study, provide a public forum for the promotion of alternative transportation, and serve as a resource for alternative transportation project implementation.

The committee would pursue projects that enhance traveler mobility, develop cost savings, and create greater visibility for alternative transportation. These projects may include, exploring the potentially underutilized private resources, improving coordination of existing and future transportation services, and expanding the dissemination of traveler information. For example, an alternative transportation technical advisory committee could facilitate a program among private ski areas and the WMNF, or another partner like AMC. Ski areas use their shuttle vehicles mainly during winter, while the WMNF peak season is during the summer and fall foliage season. An arrangement that shares vehicles among partners could provide low-cost opportunities for improving transit options through the WMNF.

In addition, the committee could aid in the joint marketing of transportation opportunities as they relate to commercial and recreational sites in the WMNF region. The committee could work with existing networks like the White Mountains Attractions, and the NH DRED to better publicize traveler information for the benefit of visitors and residents. This concept is described further in *6.2 Scenario 1 - Alternative transportation technical advisory committee.*

Scenario 1 is compatible with the transportation management improvements and could provide a foundation for the other scenarios described in this report. Table 10 lists the options included in this scenario. Table 11 lists options related to this scenario.

Table 10 - Options comprising Scenario 1 – Alternative transportation technical advisory committee.

Option ID	Option description
PP_01	Create an Alternative Transportation Technical Advisory Committee for the WMNF region.
PP_02	Improve coordination with White Mountain Attractions and encourage WMA to host car-free traveler information.
PP_03	Improve coordination with DRED Division of Travel and Tourism Development to i) include more information about WMNF on the visitnh.gov website and ii) host car-free traveler information to the region.
PP_04	Improve coordination with North Country Council to expand transportation planning efforts in the region to consider needs of recreational visitors and car-free travel for recreational purposes.
PP_08	Explore opportunities for vehicle sharing with ski resorts that run winter shuttle systems.
PP_10	Explore opportunities to partner with the North Country Scenic Byways Council on projects related to the White Mountains Trail and the Kancamagus Scenic Byway- and potentially other designated trails in the area.
PP_13	Create a Friends Group to manage aspects of WMNF visitor experience.

Table 11 - Options related to Scenario 1 – Alternative Transportation Technical Advisory Committee.

Option ID	Option description
PP_12	Improve tour bus management with private operators that visit WMNF (e.g. require Special Use Permits for tour vehicles, or include tour bus operators in the Forest Service's Outfitter Guide Program).
PP_14	Create a National Forest Interpreter Program and include an interpretive service on potential transit routes to increase the value of transit among visitors.

6.3 Scenario 2 - Improved traveler information

This scenario builds on the online resources provided by AMC[18] and NH Department of Resources and Economic Development[19], and envisions a centralized, independent, non-profit traveler information resource for recreational visitors to the WMNF region, modeled in part after Cape Cod's SmartGuide[20]. Although all forms of transportation should be covered, this resource will highlight, on a single website, all regional alternative transportation options. Alternative transportation options include bicycle, pedestrian, and interstate, regional, and local transit options. Information would include the following items:

- Routes, schedules, and connections of transit providers;
- Maps of bicycle and pedestrian routes and paths;
- Locations of bicycle infrastructure and amenities; and
- Locations of park and ride lots.

---

[18] http://www.outdoors.org/conservation/transportation/index.cfm and http://www.outdoors.org/lodging/lodging-shuttle.cfm
[19] http://visitnh.gov/planning-and-travel-tools/transportation.aspx
[20] http://www.smartguide.org/

All of these materials would be available in PDF and printed forms, and printed brochures including time tables, maps, and written information would be distributed to attractions and service providers (such as resorts, hotels, restaurants, and sightseeing and tourist attractions) for the benefit of visitors to the area.

The traveler information resource would require the input and support of a variety of stakeholders in the region including North Country Transit, North Country Council, NH Department of Resources and Economic Development, NHDOT, White Mountains Attractions, C&J Bus Company, Concord Coach Lines, local towns, and resorts.

An optional component to this scenario could be the participation of interstate, regional, and local transit providers with Google Transit. Travelers from as far away as Boston would be able to use Google Transit to plan a door-to-door transit trip all the way to a specific destination in or around the White Mountains, and the traveler information website would provide an interface to this trip planning tool.

Another optional component would be an RSS feed of transit service delays due to damage, weather, or construction.

All partners would create links from their websites to this joint website. The partnership will fund a part time position i) to keep the website updated and ii) to share information about the travel resource with service providers in the region.

Funding needs include initial design and development, as well as ongoing maintenance of the resource.

Table 12 lists the options included in this scenario. Table 13 lists options related to this scenario.

Table 12 - Options comprising Scenario 2 – Improved traveler information.

Option ID	Option description
TI_01	Develop and market a web-based travel information resource to and through WMNF that includes car-free travel information and place-based traveler information in relation to local recreational opportunities.
TI_02	Implement a "travel trainer" program to educate travel, tourism, and recreation partners (e.g. member of White Mountain Attractions, resorts/hotels, business owners, etc.) about alternative travel opportunities in and around WMNF.
TI_03	Provide local establishments with information about car-free recreation opportunities.
TR_10	Designate and promote Park and Ride lots in the White Mountain region under the NH DOT Rideshare program.
TR_11	Promote scheduling coordination with regional and local public and private transportation providers.

Table 13 - Options related to Scenario 2 – Improved traveler information.

Option ID	Option description
PP_01	Create an Alternative Transportation Technical Advisory Committee for the WMNF region.
BP_01	Improve bicycling/pedestrian infrastructure (e.g. crosswalks, designated bicycle parking, wayfinding signage, information, concessions, and secured lockers) at recreational sites in the WMNF (e.g. Day Use areas/campgrounds, trail heads) and at major lodging access nodes (e.g. surrounding towns/areas, resorts, etc.).
TR_01	Develop a tour/shuttle route on the Kancamagus Highway during peak visitation.

6.4   Scenario 3 - Bicycle and pedestrian infrastructure

This option improves the bicycle and pedestrian amenities and infrastructure provided in and around the WMNF. Improving bicycle and pedestrian infrastructure encompasses two general efforts:

- Providing amenities at destinations; and
- Improving access among destinations.

Bicycle and pedestrian amenities at destinations include crosswalks, designated bicycle parking or secured bicycle lockers, wayfinding signage, information, and concessions. Increasing access among destinations includes constructing new bicycle and pedestrian paths, or bicycle lanes, and improving wayfinding signage. Bicycle and pedestrian features are often complementary, for example cyclists may use crosswalks to facilitate safe travel movements, and directional signage is useful too all travelers. Providing these features at and around the WMNF legitimizes and encourages cycling and walking. All bicycle and pedestrian improvements in and around the WMNF should be designed and implemented using Complete Street and Universal Design concepts.

Providing amenities at destinations

Pedestrian and bicycle amenities at WMNF locations are minimal and could be improved in the surrounding towns. Currently, no trailheads within the WMNF are equipped with bicycle racks. WMNF could install bicycle racks at popular trail heads and explore the use of Recreational Enhancement Act fees to cover the capital and maintenance costs associated with the improvements. WMNF could implement this change quickly, and at relatively low cost. Additional or more complex amenities like wayfinding signage or concessions at major destinations could be implemented through a long-term phased approach and financed through existing Forest Service funding, through a public-private partnership model, or other means. In addition, WMNF could encourage local municipalities to improve pedestrian and bicycle amenities in commercial and recreational locations.

Improving access to WMNF destinations

Improving access to WMNF destinations could include adding on-road bicycle lanes, extending existing or constructing new off-road paths, and/or improving way finding signage. Several NHDOT designated bicycle routes run through the WMNF,[21] and in most cases, these routes do not include bicycle symbols or bicycle lane markings. WMNF could consider working with the NHDOT to provide a clearer roadside

---

[21] NHDOT Bicycle/Pedestrian Accessed December 15, 2010. http://www.nh.gov/dot/programs/bikeped/maps/documents/wm_map.pdf.

presence of designated bicycle routes through the WMNF by creating designated bicycle lanes and installing signage to increase safety for cyclists and motorists, especially on those routes that connect major towns and WMNF recreational sites.

Several potential projects for extending existing bicycle paths or constructing new off-road bicycle and pedestrian paths could create connections between major towns and WMNF recreational areas. Four potential bicycle paths are as follows:

- A north-south extension of the existing Franconia Notch bicycle path to the Town of Lincoln;
- A bicycle path between Twin Mountain and Skookumchuck trailhead;
- A bicycle path between Twin Mountain and Bretton Woods; and
- A bicycle path between Bretton Woods and AMC Highland Center at Crawford Notch.

WMNF has completed the environmental assessment for a potential portion of a bicycle path corridor extending north- east from the Skookumchuck trailhead to the Village of Twin Mountain. A preferred alternative route has been selected, and design and construction may begin if and when funding is secured.

Projects to extend existing bicycle paths or construct new ones require a long-term partnership with the NH DOT Bicycle Pedestrian Program. Other partners could include NH Division of Parks and Recreation, NH Scenic Byways, NH Park and Ride, the Towns of Lincoln, Woodstock, Franconia, Bethlehem, and Carroll. Depending on the project type, funding sources include, NHDOT State Surface Transportation Enhancement, TRIP, and potentially other sources.

This alternative is compatible with *6.7 Scenario 6 - WMNF front country infrastructure improvements* and several other options described in this report. Table 14 lists the options included in this scenario. Table 15 lists options related to this scenario, which improve traveler information, transit service, road safety, and promote ATS through the WMNF.

Table 14 - Options comprising Scenario 3 – Bicycle and pedestrian infrastructure.

Option ID	Option description
BP_01	Improve bicycling/pedestrian infrastructure (e.g. crosswalks, designated bicycle parking, wayfinding signage, information, concessions, and secured lockers) at recreational sites in the WMNF (e.g. Day Use areas/campgrounds, trail heads) and at major lodging access nodes (e.g. surrounding towns/areas, resorts, etc.).
BP_02	Improve non-motorized access (e.g. extend existing, or construct new on-road and off-road, paved and non-paved trails) between recreational sites in the WMNF (e.g. Day Use areas/campgrounds) and at major lodging access nodes (e.g. surrounding towns/areas, resorts, etc.).
BP_03	Extend the Franconia Recreation Bike Path to AMC Highland Center/Town of Lincoln.
BP_04	Construct a bicycle path between Twin Mountain and Bretton Woods.
BP_05	Construct a bicycle path between Twin Mountain and Skookumchuck trailhead.
BP_06	Relocate trailheads to consolidate access points.
BP_07	Add crosswalks in high pedestrian/bicycle travel areas.

Table 15 - Options related to Scenario 3 – Bicycle and pedestrian infrastructure.

Option ID	Option description
TI_01	Develop and market a web-based travel information resource to and through WMNF that includes car-free travel information and place-based traveler information in relation to local recreational opportunities
TI_02	Implement a "travel trainer" program to educate travel, tourism, and recreation partners (e.g. member of White Mountain Attractions, resorts/hotels, business owners, etc.) about alternative travel opportunities in and around WMNF
TI_03	Provide local establishments with information about car-free recreation opportunities
TI_04	Identify and work to implement roadway signage in specific problem areas (e.g. Bear Notch Road seasonal road closure information).
TR_04	Develop a transit/shuttle/bicycle trailer service to popular bicycle loops.
TR_10	Designate and promote Park-and-Ride lots in the White Mountain region under the NH DOT Rideshare program
PP_01	Create an Alternative Transportation Technical Advisory Committee for the WMNF region.
PP_02	Improve coordination with White Mountain Attractions and encourage WMA to host car-free traveler information.
PP_03	Improve coordination with DRED Division of Travel and Tourism Development to i) include more information about WMNF on the visitnh.gov website and ii) host car-free traveler information to the region.
PP_09	Conduct roadway safety audit to investigate widening road shoulders for cyclists, reducing speed limits, improving pedestrian crossings, and identifying pavement repairs.

6.5 Scenario 4 - AMC shuttle service expansion

The AMC shuttle system successfully serves patrons of AMC huts, as described in *4.5.1 Transit inventory*, and there may be opportunities to expand the system to serve a wider community of hikers and recreationists.

This scenario expands on the current AMC shuttle system by adding more stops along existing routes, connecting with other transportation services in the region, particularly at fixed-route nodes, increasing the frequency or range of service by adding one or more shuttle vehicles to its fleet, installing bike racks on its shuttle vehicles to accommodate cyclists, and/or extending routes to reach a greater number of trailheads or recreation venues.

WMNF could assist the shuttle system by supplying vehicles, either through its existing GSA fleet contract, or perhaps with money from a TRIP grant. WMNF could also aid with other capital investments such as bus shelters and signage at bus stops including posted routes and schedules. Revenues from ticket sales would attempt to recover only operations and maintenance costs to break-even.

AMC and WMNF could market the service by advertising one-way hiking itineraries of varying lengths and difficulties that the shuttle would enable. They could also advertise the driver as an information source who shares good spots for hiking, picnicking, swimming, photography, or wildlife viewing.

Additional shuttles could be added in key corridors on peak autumn weekends to accommodate increased demand by tourists and day-trippers.

Table 16 lists the options included in this scenario. Table 17 lists options related to this scenario.

Table 16 - Options comprising Scenario 4 – AMC shuttle service expansion.

Option ID	Option description
TR_03	Extend AMC hiker shuttle, to Conway / North Conway / Lincoln or to other hubs / nodes.

Table 17 - Options related to Scenario 4 – AMC shuttle service expansion.

Option ID	Option description
TR_02	Develop a transit service from Lincoln to the Franconia State Park area to connect with the Franconia bike path.
TR_08	Develop a transportation hub/center for regional bus travelers located primary in Lincoln/Conway/N.Conway or secondary in Littleton/Gorham/Plymouth/Campton/Franconia/Twin Mountain.
TR_10	Designate and promote Park and Ride lots in the White Mountain region under the NH DOT Rideshare program.
PP_10	Expand and enforce recreational fee structure and explore as a means to fund ATS within WMNF.
PP_11	Explore opportunities to partner with the North Country Scenic Byways Council on projects related to the White Mountains Trail and the Kancamagus Scenic Byway- and potentially other designated trails in the area.

6.6 Scenario 5 - Shuttle service on the Kancamagus Highway

This scenario seeks to relieve congestion and illegal roadway shoulder parking by introducing limited seasonal shuttle service on the Kancamagus Highway among high use sites, including visitor information centers, campgrounds, developed day use sites, popular trailheads, a WMNF District Ranger Station, and retail and service establishments in Lincoln and Conway. The service would be operated by Tri-Cap or other regional transit operator, and vehicles would be leased from one or more local ski resorts whose bus fleets are idle during the skiing offseason.

The service would run four peak weekends during the autumn season from 10 am to 4 pm, hours during which the Kancamagus Highway would be closed to vehicles with out-of-state license plates. Visitors with out-of-state license plates could park their cars in the towns of Lincoln and Conway, visit the local establishments, and gather at bus stops to catch the shuttle buses. Shops and service establishments would be asked to allow visitors to park cars in their parking lots, with the idea that visitors may visit their establishments. The towns may choose to take advantage of the concentration of visitors by hosting a series of autumn-themed fairs on these days.

Buses would run every fifteen minutes between Lincoln and Conway via the Kancamagus Highway. Passengers would pay a single transportation fare, between $5 and $10 (depending on the cost of operating the system), to hop on and off the bus as many times as they wish in a given day. The WMNF recreation fee of $3 would be waived for those visitors using the transit service. WMNF would provide a volunteer interpreter on each shuttle vehicle to explain the history, cultural, and ecology of the region to passengers, as well as make suggestions as to what types of activities and sights may be best suited for individual visitor groups.

Signs with the shuttle route and schedule would be placed at each stop along the route. Pedestrian shelters could be constructed at particularly high use sites to protect waiting passengers from the elements.

Table 18 lists the options included in this scenario. Table 19 lists options related to this scenario.

Table 18 - Options comprising Scenario 5 – Shuttle service on the Kancamagus.

Option ID	Option description
TR_01	Develop a tour/shuttle route on the Kancamagus Highway during peak visitation.

Table 19 - Options related to Scenario 5 – Shuttle service on the Kancamagus.

Option ID	Option description
TR_08	Develop a transportation hub/center for regional bus travelers located primary in Lincoln/Conway/N.Conway or secondary in Littleton/Gorham/Plymouth/Campton/Franconia/Twin Mountain.
TR_10	Designate and promote Park and Ride lots in the White Mountain region under the NH DOT Rideshare program.
PP_10	Expand and enforce recreational fee structure and explore as a means to fund ATS within WMNF.
PP_11	Explore opportunities to partner with the North Country Scenic Byways Council on projects related to the White Mountains Trail and the Kancamagus Scenic Byway- and potentially other designated trails in the area.

6.7 Scenario 6 - WMNF front country infrastructure improvements

This scenario provides a strategy to provide better pedestrian and bicycle access among WMNF Front Country sites by consolidating trail access points with existing parking areas to more efficiently manage visitor parking and create potential future shuttle stops. Front country sites are recreational sites like day use picnic areas or camping areas accessible from forest roads, as opposed to back country sites that are generally not accessible by motorized transportation. These sites generate a higher frequency of parking turnover, as visitors stays may vary from a few hours to several days.

WMNF infrastructure improvements would create an interconnected system of non-motorized trails that converge at parking hubs, as a means to reduce motorized trips among WMNF sites by allowing visitors to park once, and then walk or bicycle to other locations in the forest. Types of enhancements include:

- Extending existing hiking trails to meet with existing parking areas;

- Constructing new on-road or off-road paths to make non-motorized connections with existing parking areas;
- Re-locating parking areas closer to existing trailheads; or
- Re-locating and/or consolidating trailheads.

This scenario builds from the analysis of approximately 380 WMNF trailheads and activity sites, and the identification of 26 opportunities for infrastructure improvements at or between these areas. From this analysis, the WMNF could make several pedestrian improvements that are less than one mile in length. The construction of new, or extensions of existing bicycle paths ranged from one to five miles in length. For more detailed information see *4.8 WMNF recreational infrastructure analysis*. Implementation of these projects could be done by the WMNF alone, or in partnership with other agencies. Potential partners include, NHDOT, the surrounding towns of Lincoln, Conway, Twin Mountains, and others, and regional planning entities like the North Country Council.

This scenario is closely related to *6.4 Scenario 3 - Bicycle and pedestrian infrastructure*, but focuses specifically on non-motorized access among sites within the WMNF. Table 20 lists the options included in this scenario. Table 21 lists options related to this scenario, which improve bicycle and pedestrian amenities and access at sites in the WMNF and in the surrounding communities.

Table 20 - Options comprising Scenario 6 – WMNF front country infrastructure improvements.

Option ID	Option description
BP_06	Relocate WMNF trailheads to consolidate access points.
BP_07	Add crosswalks in high pedestrian/bicycle travel areas.
PP_07	Quantitatively identify high use recreational areas to aid in ATS planning efforts as a means to improve access management to trails and natural features.

Table 21 - Options related to Scenario 6 – WMNF front country infrastructure improvements.

Option ID	Option description
BP_01	Improve bicycling/pedestrian infrastructure (e.g. crosswalks, designated bicycle parking, wayfinding signage, information, concessions, and secured lockers) at recreational sites in the WMNF (e.g. Day Use areas/campgrounds, trail heads) and at major lodging access nodes (e.g. surrounding towns/areas, resorts, etc.).
BP_02	Improve non-motorized access (e.g. extend existing, or construct new on-road and off-road, paved and non-paved trails) between recreational sites in the WMNF (e.g. Day Use areas/campgrounds) and at major lodging access nodes (e.g. surrounding towns/areas, resorts, etc.).
BP_03	Extend the Franconia Recreation Bike Path to AMC Highland Center/Town of Lincoln.
BP_04	Construct a bicycle path between Twin Mountain and Bretton Woods
BP_05	Construct a bicycle path between Twin Mountain and Skookumchuck trailhead
PP_09	Conduct roadway safety audit to investigate widening road shoulders for cyclists, reducing speed limits, improving pedestrian crossings, and identifying pavement repairs.

7   Next steps / recommendations

This study effort to examine alternative transportation options for the WMNF was a collaborative effort built on the foundation of previous transportation studies. The study team created study goals, research ATS at other similar public lands, reviewed transportation existing conditions at WMNF, examined possible non-motorized infrastructure improvements at trailheads and other popular sites in the forest, and recommended locations for additional permanent traffic counters with which to learn more about visitor use patterns. The study team documented the area's transportation issues in four categories, including the following: traveler Information / wayfinding / signage; bicycle and pedestrian; transit; and policy and planning. Using these same four categories, the study team devised transportation options to address those issues. The team then bundled options together to create several possible scenarios for alternative transportation outcomes. Throughout the entire process the study team presented ideas to and received feedback from key stakeholders in the region. The results are documented in this final report.

Although this study effort is now over, the real work toward improving alternative transportation is just beginning, and this final report shall be a guide for the WMNF and its stakeholders to take short term and long term steps toward that goal.

The study team recommends the following next steps:

- **Establish and improve relationships among regional transportation stakeholders.** Many of the options and scenarios described in this report would require successful partnerships, and the transportation management improvements and scenarios described above provide several suggestions for ways to work with regional transportation partners. For example, WMNF and its stakeholders can participate in existing transportation committees and planning efforts, including regional and statewide transportation planning. Eventually, they may seek to create an alternative transportation technical advisory committee. Establishing new and improving existing partnerships will be central to improving transportation in and around the forest.
- **Enlarge the significance of transportation in updates to the Forest Plan.** The 2005 Forest Plan mentions transportation but provides few goals, objectives, or strategies related to access, mobility, efficiency, resource protection, congestion, parking, bicycling, walking, wayfinding, or traveler information. Addressing these issues in the Forest Plan may provide policy direction to forest staff members and stakeholders regarding alternative transportation.
- **Install permanent traffic counters.** The WMNF may install permanent traffic counters to complement those in use by NHDOT. In *4.4 Traffic analysis*, this study analyzed locations of existing traffic counters and found that most are located outside of the WMNF and collect a great deal of data about non-recreationalist road users. The study team recommends that permanent traffic counters be installed in key corridors in the forest, specifically outside of developed areas, and coordinated with New Hampshire and Maine DOTs. The availability additional traffic data will help the WMNF and departments of transportation better understand transportation dynamics in the forest and support future planning efforts.

- **Seek alternative transportation quick-wins.** While several of the concepts studied during this effort included establishing new transit systems or expanding existing ones, some of the options and scenarios identified require less effort and may have far-reaching results. For example, the transportation management improvements section includes a task of closing the existing transit service gaps documented in *5 Alternative transportation issues and options*. In addition, as part of this study, AMC has built a traveler information resource it is hosting on its website. WMNF can link to this resource from its website, and AMC can ask visitnh.gov and White Mountains Attractions to do the same. WMNF may also be able to identify some low-cost data collection efforts to improve its understanding of transportation in the forest. For example, volunteers or college students could monitor key intersections, parking lots, or tour bus activity on peak weekends and record car counts and usage patterns. Also prior to bicycle planning or bicycle amenity improvement projects, the Forest may choose to install bicycle amenities at one or two key recreation areas and observe resulting usage patterns.
- **Discuss and consider moving forward with one or more scenarios.** The six scenarios presented in this report represent visions of the study team for alternative transportation. The WMNF and stakeholders could study these scenarios in greater detail and implement them, perhaps using funding from additional TRIP grants or transportation enhancement funding. Specific TRIP application guidance for national forests may be found online.[22]
- **Use the tools created in this study to create additional scenarios.** By documenting transportation issues and options, the study team has provided tools for WMNF and its stakeholders to create new scenarios. By revisiting the issues and related options, follow-on efforts by WMNF and its stakeholders may combine bundles of options to create new scenarios.

---

[22] http://publiclands.volpe.dot.gov/usfs-alternative-transportation/index.shtm

Appendix A – Alternative transportation system peer comparison

This appendix provides detailed case study comparisons of ATS on federal lands, including a summary of key lessons and opportunities as they relate to the WMNF.

The WMNF, along with three partners,[23] is conducting an alternative transportation study to mitigate the effects of several transportation issues: 1) heavy traffic and parking overflows at peak visitation times which leads to congestion, increased emissions, and negative impacts to the visitor experience; and 2) safety hazards and resource degradation due to unauthorized parking within the forest.

To identify potential alternatives for WMNF, this memorandum describes ATS implemented by comparable public lands to identify models that may have applicability to the challenges WMNF faces. Comparisons are made based on land area, road access and configuration, population of surrounding communities, annual visitation, and major activities supported in the area.

WMNF is located in north-central New Hampshire and southwestern Maine. The forest encompasses approximately 785,000 acres of spruce and northern hardwoods and paper birch. The forest includes 157 miles of road open to passenger car travel, 1,200 miles of hiking trails, 400 miles of snowmobile trails, 160 miles of the Appalachian Trail, 23 developed campgrounds, and numerous Nordic and alpine ski areas. Approximately 1.7 million people visit WMNF each year, while between 5-7 million visitors visit and or pass through the forest or surrounding communities each year.[24] There are hundreds of disaggregated trailheads and access points within the forest that allow for, with few exceptions, dispersed visitation, as opposed to a handful of popular attractions that concentrate visitation.

Although no other place is identical to WMNF, several public lands with similar characteristics and challenges offer examples of transportation solutions that may inform dialogue during the current planning exercise. The following public lands units and their associated ATS are discussed in this memorandum:

- **The Bureau of Land Management Eagle Lake Field Office area** has dispersed visitation spread among a variety of destinations, akin the numerous trailheads within the WMNF. The now defunct partnership between the Bureau of Land Management and the local transit provider to provide transit to the Bizz Johnson trial offers lessons learned for supplying an alternative to private vehicle access to a specific trailhead destination.
- **The North Moab Recreation Areas**, including Arches National Park and the BLM Moab Field Office, consists largely of dispersed trail heads. To create opportunities for alternative transportation in the area, a transportation hub is being planned that will centralize travel destinations to a single location, and facilitate trail access by means other than private automobiles.
- **Delaware Water Gap National Recreation Area** has several main roads that experience a great deal of commuter and cut-through traffic, much like the roads in WMNF. One road and several

---

[23] The U.S. DOT Volpe Center, Plymouth State University (PSU), and the Appalachian Mountain Club (AMC)
[24] The National Visitor Use Monitoring program estimated 1,692,000 visitors to WMNF itself for FY2005.

bridges utilize tolls to mitigate traffic and fund maintenance and operations of the unit's transportation infrastructure.

- **The White River National Forest**, like WMNF, is a national forest that experiences extreme seasonal peaks in visitation. The Maroon Bells Shuttle service provides an instructive case of how this land unit partners with the local Roaring Fork Transit Authority to manage visitor demand on a single scenic road during peak season.
- **Sequoia National Park** is only several hours' drive from major urban population centers in San Francisco and Los Angeles. WMNF is a similar distance from Boston. A cooperative agreement between the park service and the city of Visalia to provide shuttle service to, and throughout the park provides a model for reducing automobile congestion and greenhouse gas emissions.
- **Zion National Park** and its transit system are tightly integrated with its gateway community, Springdale, much the same way that WMNF is symbiotic with Lincoln and Conway.
- **Acadia National Park** experiences annual visitation of approximately 2 million people. Though it is a fraction of the size of WMNF, and its island geography creates natural constraints on the travel network that serve transit well, the Island Explorer bus system provides a case study for innovative partnerships in the delivery of transit service.

Eagle Lake Field Office, Bizz Johnson Trail, California and Nevada (BLM)
ATS Type – Weekend transit service - cooperation with local transit provider, no formal agreement

The Bureau of Land Management (BLM) Eagle Lake Field Office manages public lands that cover approximately one million acres in northeastern California and northwestern Nevada. The area offers considerable diversity including forests, lakes, scenic river canyons, and expansive high deserts. Recreational opportunities in these areas include hiking, bicycling, horseback riding, while resource extraction activities include timber harvesting and livestock grazing.[25]

The Bizz Johnson Trail is approximately 25 miles of gravel and dirt recreational trail in the Eagle Lake Field area that connects directly to the towns of Susanville, CA. Susanville has a population approximately 13,500, and the adjacent Westwood, California has a population of approximately 2,000. [2] The one-way nature of the Bizz Johnson Trail lends itself well to a shuttle service, whereby users could park their cars at one end, ride a shuttle to the other end, and bike back to their origin. A private shuttle operator currently provides on-demand service of this nature, and, the, Lassen Rural Bus (LRB), a transit service operating in Lassen County, provides weekday bus service with three daily trips, stopping at or near several trail access points. The bus is equipped with racks to carry up to two bicycles.

In 2006, Eagle Lake staff recognized the visitor demand for a low-cost weekend shuttle and initiated a partnership between the BLM and LRB. Between 2006 and 2009 LRB carried passengers and BLM provided a vehicle towing a utility trailer to carry up to 20 bicycles to the Bizz Johnson Trail. The service was offered one weekend day per month during the peak fall season. The BLM marketed the service and provided some operations assistance, while the LRB provided the bus for passengers, and a driver. Visitors rode the Lassen bus, shown in Figure 36, for a small fee that paid LRB for the cost of operating

---

[25] Bureau of Land Management, Eagle Creek Office. Accessed July 14, 2010. http://www.blm.gov/ca/st/en/fo/eaglelake/blmfacts.html
[2] U.S. Census 2000.

the bus. BLM promoted the shuttle in local and regional news releases and assisted in the hauling of bicycles by providing vehicles or trailers. During the shuttle ride, a BLM interpreter provided natural, historical and visitor information to visitors.[3]

Currently, because of conflicts with Federal Charter Bus regulations, that prohibit public transit agencies from providing charter services, this partnership between BLM and LRB is no longer active. However, through a recent LRB public planning process, in which the BLM participated, LRB staff recognized the need for a weekend bus to serve Susanville, and other parts of Lassen County. As a result, the LRB fixed route transit service will be extended in the fall of 2010 to weekend days. This service extension will provide hikers and cyclists access the Bizz Johnson trail on the Lassen bus, which has a capacity to carry up to two bicycles. In addition, once a year, during late October BLM, partners with LRB for the Eagle Lake Field Office's annual Fall Colors Bicycle Ride, along the Bizz Johnson trail from Westwood to Susanville. For this event, LRB returns riders and their bicycles back the BLM offices after riders complete the 25-mile ride.[4]

Figure 36 - Passengers alight from the BLM/Lassen Rural Bus shuttle. Source: Bureau of Land Management

---

[3] Bureau of Land Management. Eagle Lake Office. Annual Report, 2004. California Recreation Fee Demonstration Project Accomplishments for FY 2004
[4] Personal communication with Bureau of Land Management, Eagle Creek Office staff. August 23, 2010.

Bureau of Land Management Moab Field Office, Arches National Park, Grand County, Utah (BLM, NPS, and Grand County, UT)

ATS Type – Transit hub/welcome center/park- construction of area to concentrate transportation activities and access to recreational trails, construction partnership, no formal agreement with transportation providers

Moab, Utah has become well known as a major destination for mountain and road biking, hiking, rock climbing, rafting, and off road vehicle use that attracts visitors from all over the United States. The North Moab Recreation Areas refer to a selection of adjacent public lands including Arches National Park, the BLM Moab Field Office, and other state recreation areas. In recent years, parking shortages at trailheads and safety issues with pedestrians and bicycles along the roadways have become more common. Most visitors drive to trailheads along State Highway 191 and State Route 128, the two main roads to and through the Moab Recreation Area.

According to the National Park Service, "the North Moab Recreation Areas Alternative Transportation System is a network of non-motorized pathways and bridges and shuttle opportunities that link Moab City to Arches and Canyonlands National Parks, Dead Horse Point State Park, and thousands of acres of BLM public lands."[26] Grand County, Utah in cooperation with the BLM Moab Field Office, Arches National Park, and several other groups, devised a multi-faceted alternative transportation project to integrate the Lions Park Trail to include a Welcome Center and Transit Hub, situated at the intersection of US 191 and SR 128 as a focal point of the entire project. The project will connect extensive non-motorized paths, including a pedestrian/bicycle bridge over the Colorado River to the town of Moab to Arches National Park, BLM lands, and other public lands.[27] In 2007, a grant of $774,000 was awarded to Grand County through the ATPPL program for the construction of the Welcome Center/Transit Hub, and $100,000 grant from the National Park Service will pay for the design of Lion's Park, shown in Figure 37, to serve visitors to the area.[28] The hub will provide a staging area for providing welcome information to visitors, a park for special events, and connects to 42.5 miles of bicycle lanes and paths. The new Lions Park transit hub portion of the project will be, located on the south side of State Highway 191, to serve as a collection area for visitors arriving on private tours, shuttles, and other visitors that walk or cycle to the area. It will include a parking lot, a transit bus loading/unloading zone, and an underpass that will allow bikers from Moab a direct connection to the area, without having to cross over a busy area road. The hub will provide direct access to an extensive trail network and will facilitate travel to the area by means other than the private vehicle. The project draws upon existing transportation providers in Moab to centralize transportation services as a means to increase access to recreational lands. The Lions Park Transit Hub is currently being developed in partnership with the National Park Service, Grand County, Moab City, the Bureau of Land Management, the Moab Trails Alliance, and others.[29] The completion of

---

[26] Lions Park Trail and Transit Hub, North Moab Recreation Areas Alternative Transportation System. Briefing, Moab Trails Alliance. September 23, 2009

[27] Guide to Promoting Bicycling on Public Lands. http://drusilla.hsrc.unc.edu/cms/downloads/01_promoting_bicycling_entire_document.pdf Appendix B - North Moab Recreation Area and Lake Tahoe Partnerships. P. 83

[28] Hatch Announces Three Transportation Grants for Utah National Parks. October 16, 2007. Accessed July 24, 2010.
<http://hatch.senate.gov/public/index.cfm?FuseAction=PressReleases.View&PressRelease_id=cf8b328c-31f9-4ac5-9b5e-0276378d1d36>

[29] National Park Service. Rivers, Trails, Conservation, and Assistance Program, Intermountain Region. Utah News. Accessed July 30, 2010. www.nps.gov/ncrc/programs/rtca/whatwedo/projects/UT.pdf

the entire project will enhance travel conditions for both motorized and non-motorized users by separating cyclists and pedestrians from vehicular traffic along the US191 corridors. In addition, the construction of the Lions Park Trail and Transit Hub at the junction of the area's two busiest highways provides the infrastructure needed to support the private shuttle system proposed in the Arches National Park Transportation Implementation Plan (2006).[30] Figure 2 illustrates the Lions Park Trail and Transportation Hub.

Figure 37 - Conceptual plan for the Lions Park Trail and Transportation Hub. Source: National Park Service

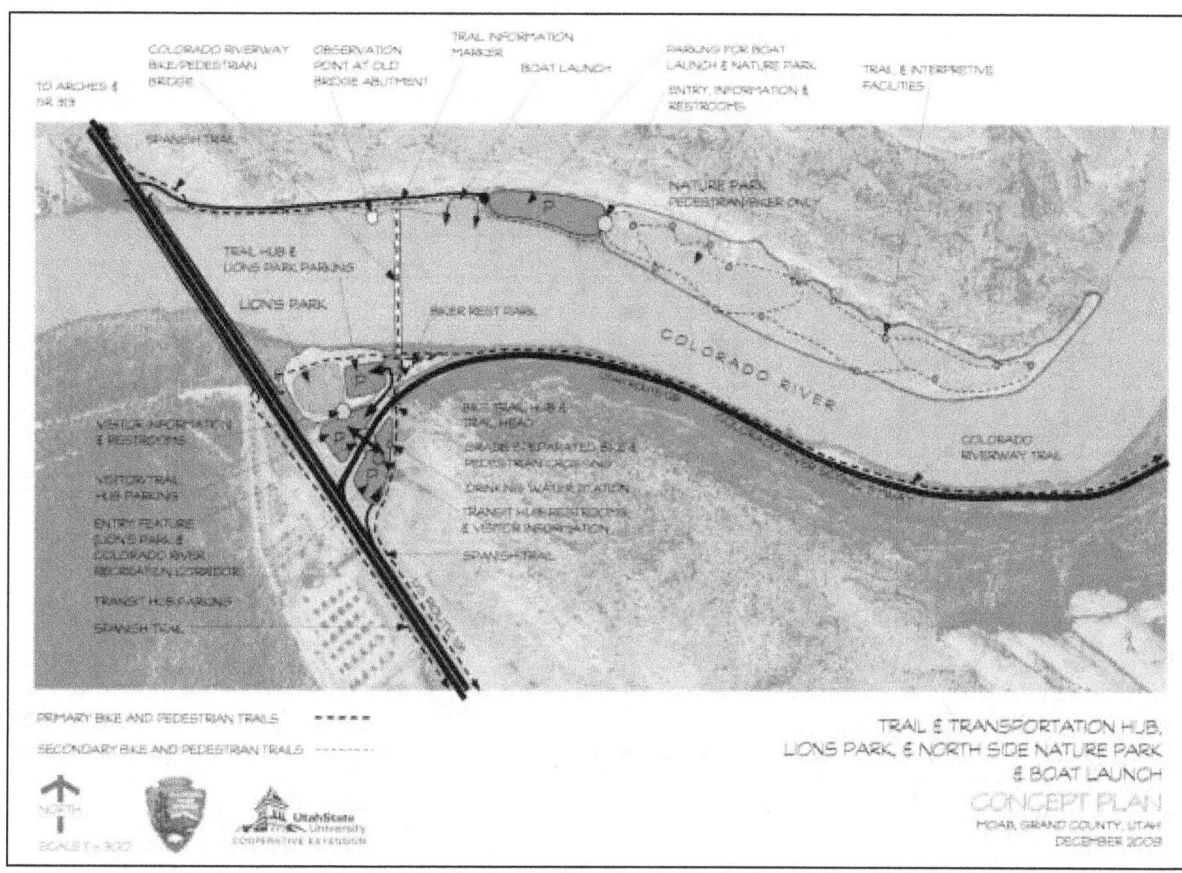

Delaware Water Gap National Recreation Area, Pennsylvania and New Jersey (NPS)

ATS Type – Communication of local transit options, no formal agreement

Delaware Water Gap National Recreation Area (DEWA), shown in Figure 38, is located in New Jersey and Pennsylvania, along 37 miles of the Delaware River, and receives over five million annual visitors. The park covers 269 acres and includes over 100 miles of trails along streams, ridges, and mountains, 27 miles of the Appalachian Trail, and over 200 miles of scenic roads. A portion of U.S. 209 runs through the

---

[30] Lions Park Trail and Transit Hub, North Moab Recreation Areas Alternative Transportation System. Briefing, Moab Trails Alliance. September 23, 2009

park with a speed limit between 35 and 45 MPH. On the section of the route that traverses the park, there are restrictions to commercial traffic between Bushkill, PA and Milford, PA.

Commercial restrictions were instituted in 1983 when the Commonwealth of Pennsylvania transferred ownership of 21 miles of U.S. 209 to NPS. NPS sought to close this road to commercial traffic, pursuant to Section 5.6 of Title 36 Code of Federal Regulations which prohibits the use of roads within National Park areas by commercial through-traffic. Due to negative outcry from the trucking industry, NPS established a commercial operation fee for certain commercial vehicles excepted from the closure. A fee booth at each end of the route regulates approximately 100 to 120 commercial vehicles that travel through the park daily31. Two major roadways also border the park, Interstate 84 to the north, and Interstate 80 to the south. Fees contribute toward the management, operation, maintenance, and construction of the road. Figure 38 illustrates the regional location of the Delaware Water Gap National Recreation Area.

Figure 38 - Delaware Water Gap National Recreation Area. Source: National Park Service

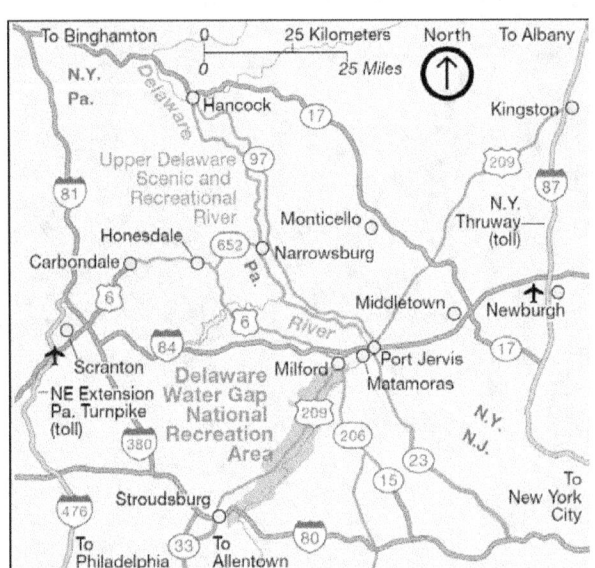

DEWA neither owns nor operates transit within the recreation area, nor does it have formal service agreement with the local transit provider in the area. Instead, connecting transit information and travel options to and through the area are detailed on the DEWA website. Bus service between New York City and Scranton, Wilkes-Barre, and the town of Delaware Water Gap, Pennsylvania, pass through DEWA. The Delaware Water Gap/Martz bus terminal is one-and-one-half and three miles from two Appalachian Trail spur trailheads, respectively. On its website, the park provides public transit and walking directions from the bus terminal to these trailheads and other park sites to facilitate car-free travel to the area. Monroe County Transit Authority also provides weekend bus service to bus terminal.

---

[31] Personal communication with Delaware Water Gap National Recreation Area staff. January 25, 2010.and unpublished NPS document, *United States Department of the Interior, National Park Service LEGISLATIVE RECOMMENDATION, Management of U.S. Route 209 through Delaware Water Gap National Recreation Area.*

Buses have bicycle racks that allow park visitors to travel by bus, in order to cycle or walk from the bus station to the park. However, visitors traveling by public transportation must be willing and able to walk or cycle between two and five miles to access the park because shuttle connections are absent between DEWA and rail and bus systems in the surrounding communities. DEWA is preparing to explore alternative transportation options in the park, one of which may be addition of a public transit route operated by the Monroe County Transit Authority.[32]

White River National Forest, Colorado (USFS)

ATS Type – Shuttle system - partnership with local transit provider, formal agreement

White River National Forest (WRNF) is one of the most popular national forests for recreation in the nation. It is located on 2.3 million acres in the Rocky Mountains and is home to world-renowned ski resorts and the Maroon Bells, the most photographed mountain peaks in North America. The city of Aspen, located within a few miles of the WRNF visitor center is a popular seasonal visitor destination with a year round population of less than 15,000 permanent residents that grows to roughly 25,000 during the peak winter season.[33] Annually, there are over 100,000 visitors to Maroon Bells.[34]

Since the 1970's private motor vehicle access to the Maroon Bells Scenic Area has been restricted during the peak season from mid-June to September. During this time, the mandatory Maroon Bells shuttle bus system, shown in

Figure 39, operates from the Aspen Highlands Ski Area with free connecting shuttle bus service from the Rubey Park Transportation Center in Aspen. Visitors park for free at the Aspen Highlands Ski Area to board the shuttle. Buses run every day from mid-June to September from 9 a.m. to 5 p.m. When the shuttle is not in operation, a recreation use fee of $10 per vehicle (good for entry into the park for five consecutive days) is charged between the hours of 9:00am – 5:00pm May 28 through June 18, and in days in September when the bus system is not operating. In September, buses operate only on Friday, Saturday, Sunday, and the seasonal bus service ends on October 1st. Vehicles can access the road before and after the hours the 9 a.m. to 5 p.m., but are encouraged to pay a voluntary "use fee".[35] Visitors arriving by vehicle with a baby in a car seat, a handicap designated license plate or placard, overnight backpackers, and campers are exempted from riding the mandatory shuttle when in operation, but still must pay the $10 recreation use fee. Cyclists and pedestrians may travel on the same scenic roadway as the shuttle and pay no entry charge for the area.[36]

---

[32] *Ibid.*

[33] Federal Highway Administration, Office of Operations. Mitigating Traffic Congestion – The Role of Demand-Side Strategies. Accessed July 24, 2010. < http://ops.fhwa.dot.gov/publications/mitig_traf_cong/aspen_case.htm>

[34] John A. Volpe National Transportation Systems Center. 1 US Forest Service TRIP Program Webinar Series.

[35] Personal communication with White River National Forest Staff. July 20, 2010.

[36] Maroon Bells Scenic Area, Aspen, CO, 2010 Summer Season Information. Accessed July 23, 2010
<http://www.fs.fed.us/r2/whiteriver/rangerdistricts/aspen_sopris/mb_scenic_site/2010-VehicleAccessMaroonBells.pdf>

Figure 39 - WRNF Maroon Bells shuttle route. Source: White River National Forest

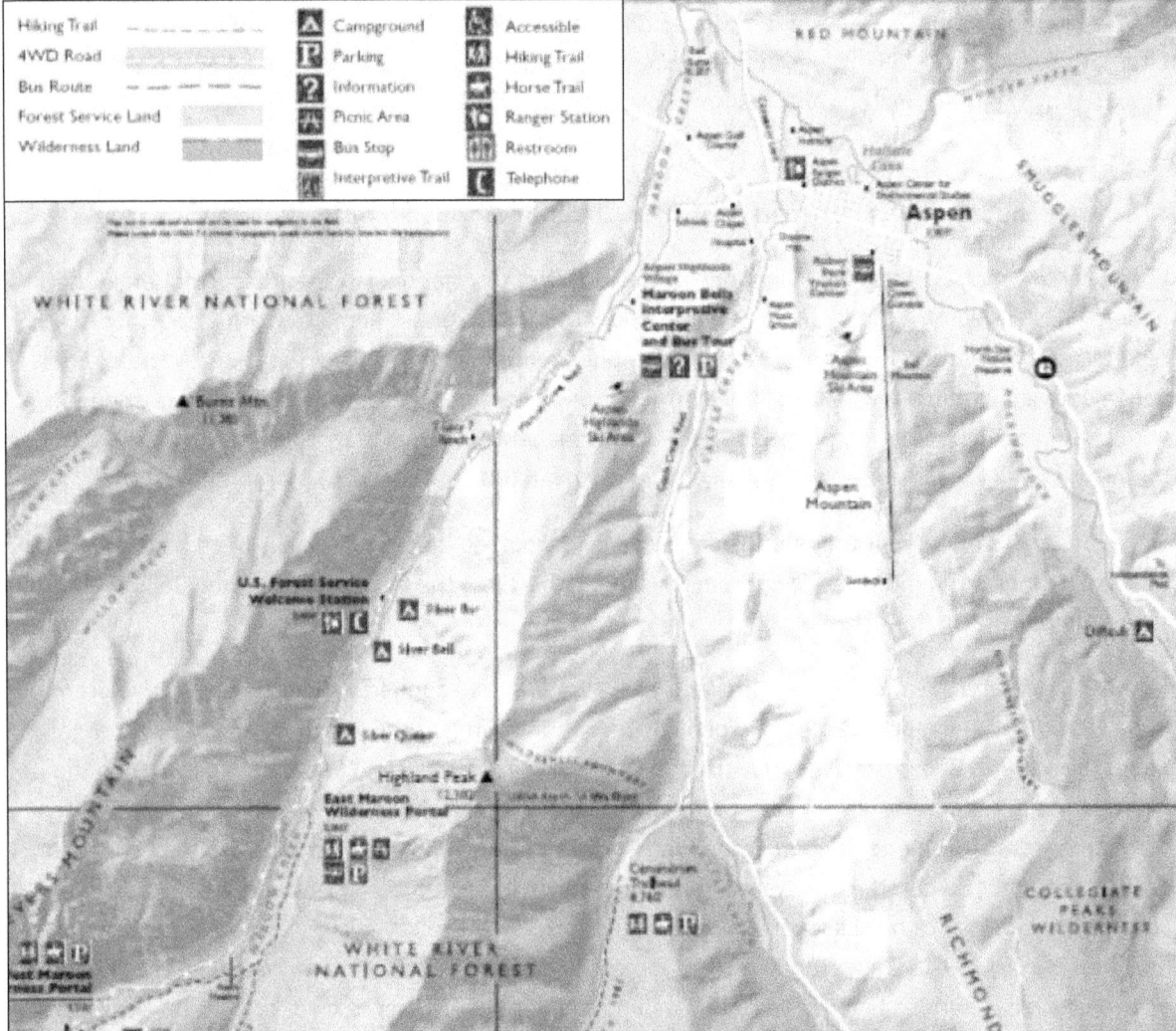

The Roaring Fork Transit Authority (RFTA) operates the Maroon Bells shuttle. RFTA operates the service in partnership with the WRNF. The cost is $6 per person, and $4 for children or seniors, and $3 for all riders on Wednesdays. Through a Memorandum of Understanding (MOU) with the forest service, RFTA owns, operates, and maintains all shuttle vehicles and provides drivers for the service. As part of the Federal Lands Recreation Enhancement Act (FLREA), fifty cents from the sale of each shuttle ticket sale, and the $10 scenic road access fee is retained by WRNF. Of these revenues, the unit retains approximately 95 percent in order to enhance visitor services which may include repair, maintenance, and facility enhancements. The Rocky Mountain Regional Forest Service office receives the remainder of the recreation fee revenues.

In 2007, RFTA and the WRNF partnered on an application to the Federal Transit Administration Alternative Transportation in Parks and Public Lands (ATPPL) program (now known as the Paul S. Sarbanes Transit in Parks, or TRIP, program) to purchase hybrid buses for the shuttle service.[37] Each shuttle can hold approximately 37 people and is equipped with racks for bicycles. In 2009, the shuttle provided 74,741 rides, with a mileage of 35,333. The seasonal peak capacity of the system is approximately 133,000 rides. The annual revenues in 2009 were $163,000, generated from ticket sales.

The primary customers on the shuttle are recreational forest visitors that want to access the Maroon Bells for day hikes. These visitors park at the Aspen Highlands and board the shuttle to access the scenic areas. Visitors riding the shuttle are coming to hike, fish, picnic, take photographs, and view wildlife and nature. Often rollerblades and cyclists will take the bus down from the Maroon Bells as a means for traveling out of the area. Visitors that use the shuttle come from all over the United States and international locations, and many riders are locals, or from the Colorado region. The primary trip origin for the shuttle is Aspen Highlands and the primary trip destination is the Maroon Bells. The peak demand time for the shuttle is 11:00 a.m. – 11:30 a.m. each day, and extra buses are added when necessary.

The key partners that coordinate the marketing of the shuttle system are the Aspen Chamber of Commerce, WRNF, and the Aspen Skiing Company. The Maroon Bells shuttle service is promoted through in a variety of ways including:

- Phone directory listings;
- Print advertisements on tourist maps, fliers and posters at all RFTA facilities;
- USFS guide and map distribution;
- Bus schedule distribution throughout Aspen;
- Co-operative promotion through Aspen Skiing Co. for combination tickets (e.g. $26 for a combination pass for Maroon Bells and Aspen Gondola ride);
- Chamber of Commerce summer Wednesday discount promotion;
- Chamber of Commerce website and information booths;
- the RFTA website;
- Concierge guides at local hotels; and
- Information clerks at Rubey Park RFTA information center in downtown Aspen.

Sequoia National Park, California (NPS)

ATS Type – Shuttle system - partnership with local transit provider, formal agreement

Sequoia National Park (Sequoia) is in the southern Sierra Nevada area, east of the city of Visalia, California. The park covers over 400,000 acres and is home to Mount Whitney, the highest point in the contiguous 48 United States. Kings Canyon National Park is north of, and adjoins with Sequoia National Park; together the units comprise over 200,000 acres of old growth forest.[38] The city of Visalia is a

---

[37] Technical Assessment of Roaring Fork Transit Authority ITS / Related Alternative Transportation Concepts on the White River National Forest. U.S. DOT Volpe National Transportation Systems Center. December 12, 2007. P.3

[38] National Park Service. Sequoia and Kings Canyons, National Parks, California. Accessed July 26, 2010. http://www.nps.gov/seki/

gateway community to the Sequoia area. Located in the San Joaquin Valley, Visalia has an estimated population of roughly 126,000[39] and is positioned between two major regional populations, San Francisco, approximately 230 miles southeast, and Los Angeles about 190 miles north. Visalia is ranked as one of the fastest growing cities in the central valley.[40]

In the early 2000's, Sequoia staff felt that the park was losing its sense of nature, and was "becoming a mini-city within a National Park."[41] In an effort to reduce the commercial elements within the park, management converted a retail market into a museum and considered methods to reduce use vehicle congestion during the peak season. Sequoia secured funding from the ATPPL/TRIP program to create a gateway shuttle to the park, as well as a shuttle within the park. NPS partnered with the city of Visalia to operate the Sequoia Shuttle beginning in the summer of 2007.[42]

The Sequoia Shuttle operates as two systems: one external system consisting of a single route connecting the city of Visalia with the park, and one internal system consisting of three routes connecting sites and attractions within the park. Though technically separate, both systems are branded similarly to provide continuity for riders.

Reservations are required for the Visalia/Sequoia Park shuttle, shown in Figure 40. It operates from May 26 through September 3 from the city of Visalia, through Three Rivers, to the Giant Forest Museum, where park visitors may transfer to the free park shuttle. The travel time between the city of Visalia and the entrance to Sequoia is approximately two hours. The shuttle runs from 7 a.m. - 9 p.m., seven days a week. The daily schedule is shown in

Figure 41. A roundtrip ticket costs $15 and includes the park entrance fee. Vehicle entrance fees, good for five days, are $20 and individual entrance fees for those traveling on foot or by bicycle, good for seven days, are $10. NPS park rangers are allowed to ride the shuttle free.

[39] California Department of Finance. Press Release: California Added 393,000 in 2009. Population tops 38.6 Million. Accessed July 26, 2010. http://www.dof.ca.gov/research/demographic/reports/estimates/e-1/2009-10/documents/E-1_2010-Press_Release.pdf
[40] *Ibid.*
[41] Personal communication with city of Visalia transit analysts for the Sequoia Shuttle. July 16, 2010.
[42] *Ibid.*

Figure 40 - Visalia/Sequoia Park shuttle route. Source: Sequoia National Park

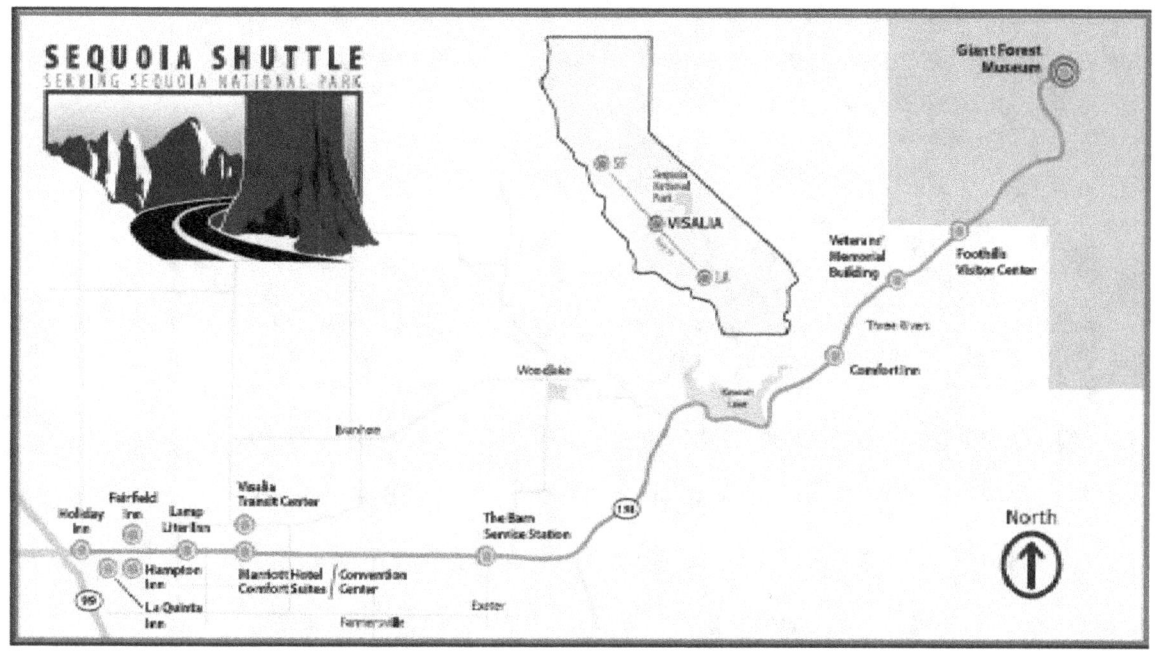

Figure 41 - Visalia/Sequoia Park route schedule, 2010. Source: Sequoia National Park

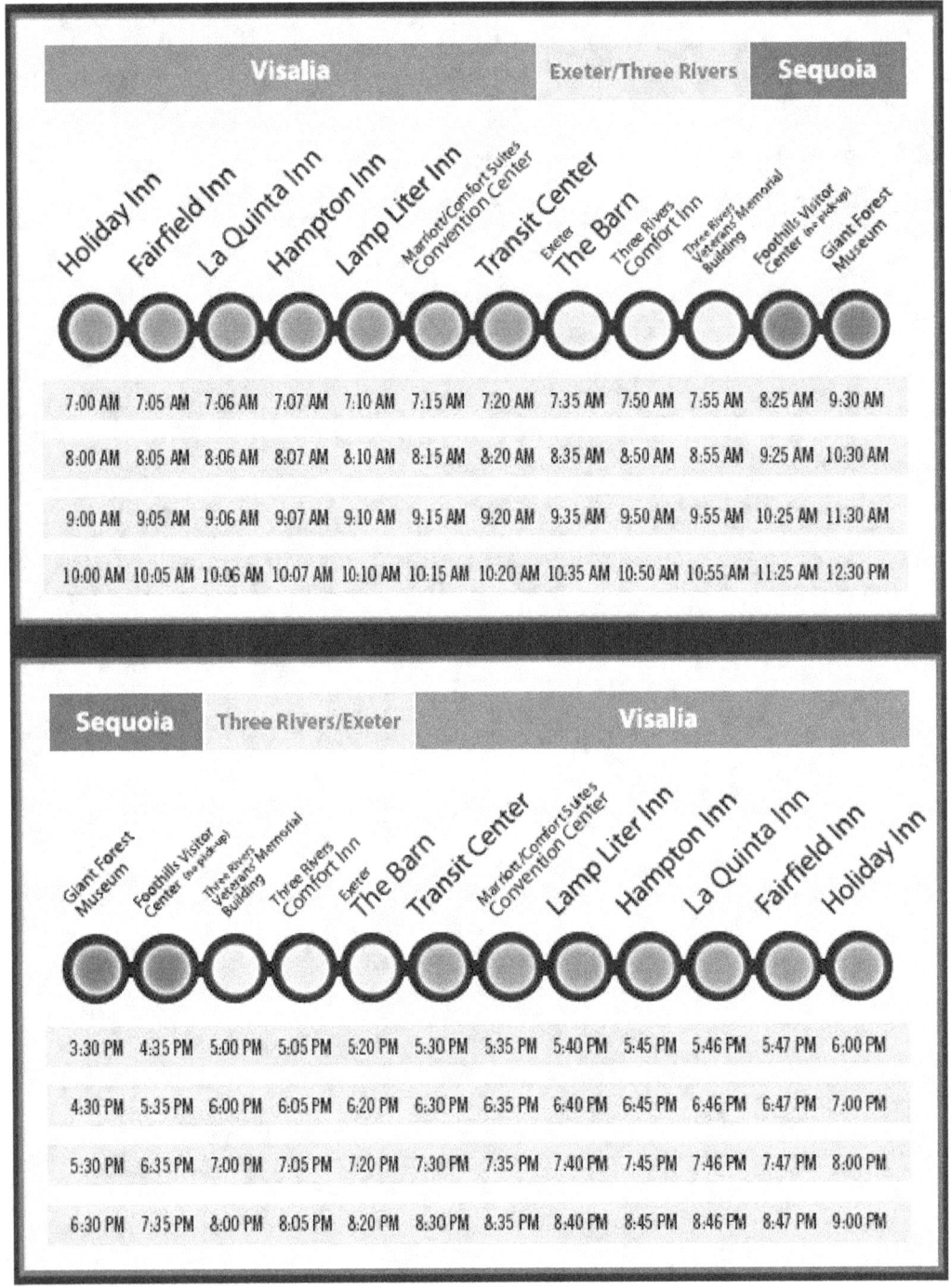

The external shuttle stops mainly at hotels (and will only stop where a reservations is made), but does include a stop at the downtown Visalia Transit Center, allowing for connections with regional bus arrivals from the surrounding areas of King County. According to 2009 pick-up location data collected by the city of Visalia, shown in Table 22, one of the most popular pick-up locations for riders is the downtown Visalia Transit Hub. The City of Visalia also has an agreement with partner hotels to allow people not lodging at the pick-up location hotels to park at in the hotel parking lot, and ride the shuttle. To date, there have been no issues with parking at any of the pick-up locations being oversubscribed due to shuttle riders.

Table 22 - Volume of pick-ups by location for Visalia / Sequoia Park route, 2009. Source: City of Visalia, Transit Division

Location	Number of pick-ups
Holiday Inn	492
Transit Center	420
Convention Center	279
Lamp Liter Inn	166
Comfort Inn	135
Memorial Building	129
Hampton Inn	91
Fairfield Inn	69
Comfort Suites	66
Marriott	45
Foothills	31
TOTAL	**1923**

The external Visalia shuttle system has nine 16 passenger vehicles and operates four vehicles Monday through Friday, and five Saturday and Sunday. All vehicles run on gasoline and feature comfortable seats, small luggage racks, bike racks, and informational videos.

The three routes that comprise the internal shuttle system, shown in Figure 42, provide fare-free service to various sites within Sequoia National Park. The Giant Forest Route, also called Route 1, or the Green Route, provides service every fifteen minutes between Giant Forest Museum, General Sherman Tree, and Lodgepole Visitor Center & campground. The Moro Rock / Crescent Meadow Route, also called Route 2, or the Gray Route, provides service every fifteen minutes between Giant Forest Museum, Moro Rock, and Crescent Meadow. The Lodgepole / Wuksachi Lodge Route, also called Route 3, or the Purple Route, provides service every thirty minutes between Lodgepole Visitor Center & Campground, Wuksachi Lodge, and Dorst Creek Campground. For visitors who arrive by car, the park suggests parking at one of the larger parking areas, such as General Sherman Tree, Lodgepole Campground Parking Area, Giant Forest Museum or Wuksachi Lodge. The park also suggests avoiding the Giant Forest Museum parking area on holiday weekends.

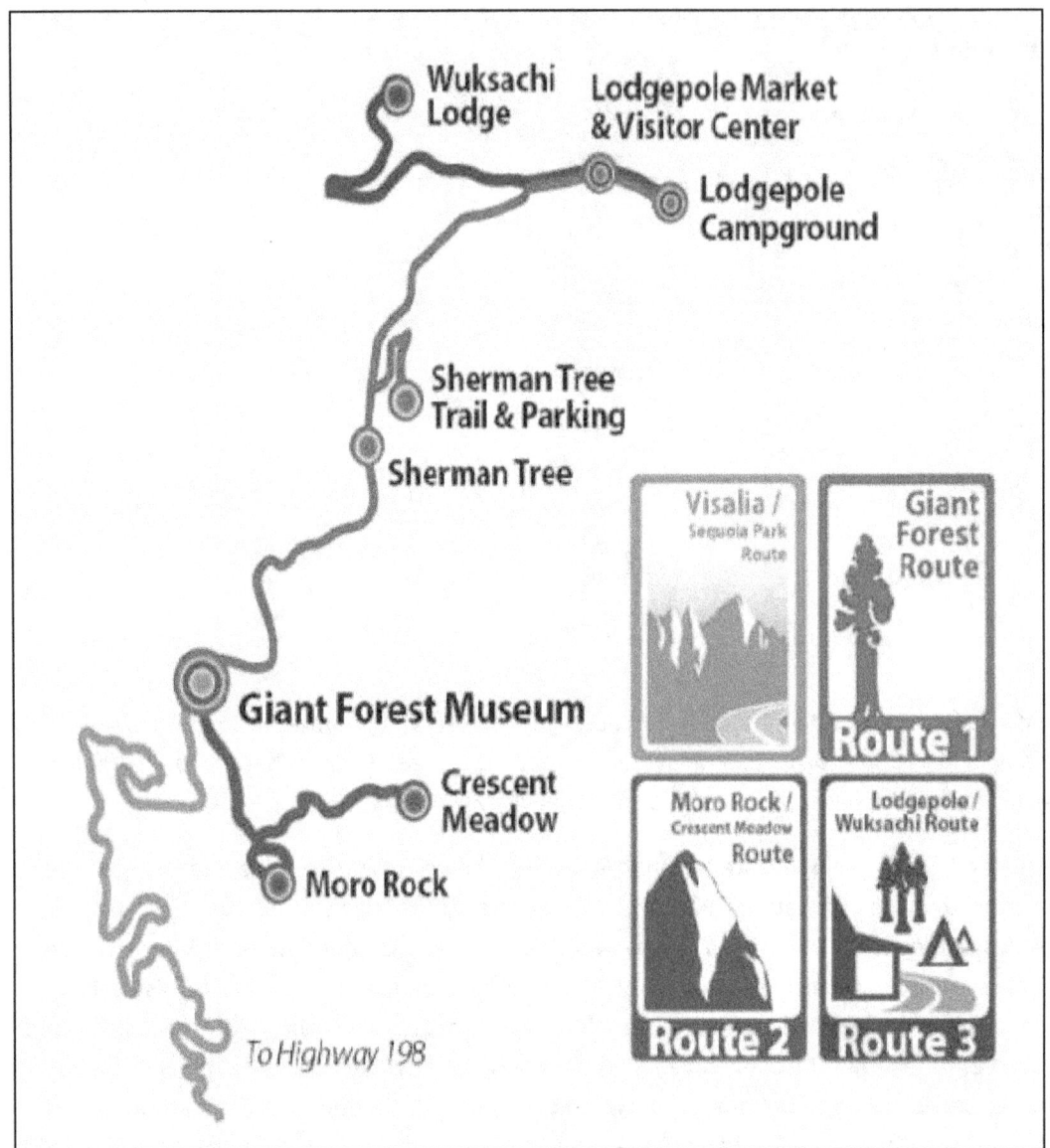

The internal Sequoia shuttle system operates six, 35 passenger vehicles, and three 16 passenger vehicles. During any given time, four of the 35 passenger vehicles are in operation, and two 16 passenger vehicles are in operation. All vehicles run on gasoline and feature comfortable seats, small luggage racks, bike racks, and an information video that plays during the trip.

The both the internal and external shuttle systems are operated under a cooperative agreement between the city of Visalia Transit division and Sequoia. The city of Visalia owns, operates and maintains the transit vehicles, provides bus drivers, and stores the vehicles after hours and during the off-season. A city of Visalia employee is assigned to oversee the daily operations of the shuttle. This manager makes regular visits to the park, to insure that the system is operating correctly, and is able to make important real time management decisions as needed. The park leases the vehicles from the City of Visalia and pays for operating expenses, including fuel costs, and provides some on-site facilities (e.g. basic maintenance tools and space), for the internal shuttle.[43]

Revenues from the system are generated through ticket sales. A $10 increase in the park entrance fee covers a portion of the internal shuttle operating expenses. In 2009, the operating costs for the internal shuttle per hour were $70, and roughly $630,000 annually. The major funding source for the capital investments for both the gateway and internal shuttle came from the ATTPL/TRIP Program. To operate the gateway shuttle the City of Visalia used Congestion Mitigation and Air Quality (CMAQ) program funding for the first three years (2007-2009) and a local economic development grant, and shuttle fares, for the fourth and fifth years (2010-2011) of operation. Financing for the future operations of the shuttle system (2012 and beyond) remain uncertain.

The system is marketed throughout the local area in print advertisements, hotel materials/brochures at concierge locations, Facebook, radio, and sometimes on television. Recently, the system offered a Groupon discount, an internet based promotional coupon, which doubled the sales of tickets in one day.[44] In addition to these efforts, visitors receive a park newspaper with shuttle information and schedule, the city of Visalia hosts a website and on-line and telephone reservation system, bus stops are posted throughout the park, and the city of Visalia and Sequoia staff utilize routine public relations and marketing activities to publicize the shuttle.

According to staff at the city of Visalia, during the first three years of operations, the shuttle operated at between 28-33 percent passenger capacity. Currently, the shuttle is running at 48 percent capacity, which the city of Visalia considers a successful target. According the NPS, the Sequoia shuttle may reduce vehicular traffic on the most popular roads throughout the forest by up to 925 cars a day. Further estimations provide that roughly 35 percent of visitors will use the shuttle, reducing emissions by up to 50 tons of pollutants per day in the area.45 This season Sequoia staff tested closing a portion of the main road through the park to vehicle traffic during select high visitation weekends that historically resulted in severe traffic congestion. As a result, traffic congestion was eliminated, and shuttle ridership increased precipitously during those days.[46]

Zion National Park, Utah (NPS)

ATS Type – Shuttle Service - NPS owned buses, operated by contractor

Zion National Park (Zion) is located in southwestern Utah, immediately adjacent to the small town of Springdale with a population of 621.[47] Springdale is largely oriented towards the tourism industry visiting Zion. The park is located approximately three hours from Las Vegas and five hours from Salt Lake City. In 2009, annual visitation was approximately 2.7 million.[48] The park is accessible by private vehicle,

---

[43] McDonald Transit Associates, Inc. Sequoia and Kings Canyon National Park, Sequoia Shuttle, Review of First Year of Operations. Draft. December 2007.

[44] Personal communication with city of Visalia transit analysts for the Sequoia Shuttle. July 16, 2010.

[45] Sequoia National Park. Accessed July 22, 2010. http://www.nps.gov/seki/planyourvisit/parktransit.htm

[46] Personal communication with City of Visalia transportation department staff.

[47] U.S. Census Bureau, Population Finder. Accessed July 14, 2010. http://www.factfinder.census.gov/

[48] National Park Service Public Use Statistics Office, Accessed July 14, 2010. <http://www.nature.nps.gov/stats/index.cfm>

commercial tour bus (with limitations during peak season) and by bicycle year-round. Zion visitors engage in activities including scenic viewing, cycling, camping, climbing, hiking, rafting, and horseback riding.

In the late 1990's, increases in visitation combined with limited parking led to recurring congestion conditions along the 6-mile upper portion of the Zion Canyon. Visitors in private automobiles on the Scenic Road would often double or triple-park along the road, destroying natural resources and diminishing the visitor experience.

In May 2000, the park implemented a seasonal shuttle bus system as a means to mitigate congestion and parking issues in the upper Zion Canyon portion of the park. The shuttle system operates fare-free during the peak visitation season, April through October. During those months, vehicles are prohibited from the scenic drive in upper portion of the Zion Canyon, unless they are registered visitors at the Zion Canyon Lodge. All other roads during peak visitation are open to private automobiles, and non-peak visitation months allow for unrestricted private vehicle access to the park. As shown in Figure 43, the park shuttle originates at the visitor center and stops at eight locations within the park, and a shuttle service operates from the town of Springdale, where it stops at six locations. The transfer point between the town shuttle and the park shuttle is at the Zion Canyon Visitor Center. The shuttle schedule and frequencies change with the season and with the time of day, and generally run every 7 minutes.[49]

The parking lot at the Visitors Center has the equivalent capacity as the parking that exists on the Zion Canyon Scenic Road of approximately 400 spaces, but typically fills by the late morning during peak months. The town of Springdale has approximately 1000 parking spaces and encourages park visitors to park their cars in town and ride the shuttle to the park free of charge. The town of Springdale directly benefits from the park shuttle system which encourages visitor spending and provides free transit service to residents. Figure 43 illustrates the Zion National Park shuttle route and stops.

---

[49] National Park Service. Zion National Park. Zion National Park. Green Transit - The Zion Shuttle. Accessed July 27, 2010.<http://www.nps.gov/zion/naturescience/green-transit-the-zion-shuttle.htm>

Figure 43 - Zion National Park Shuttle. Source: National Park Service

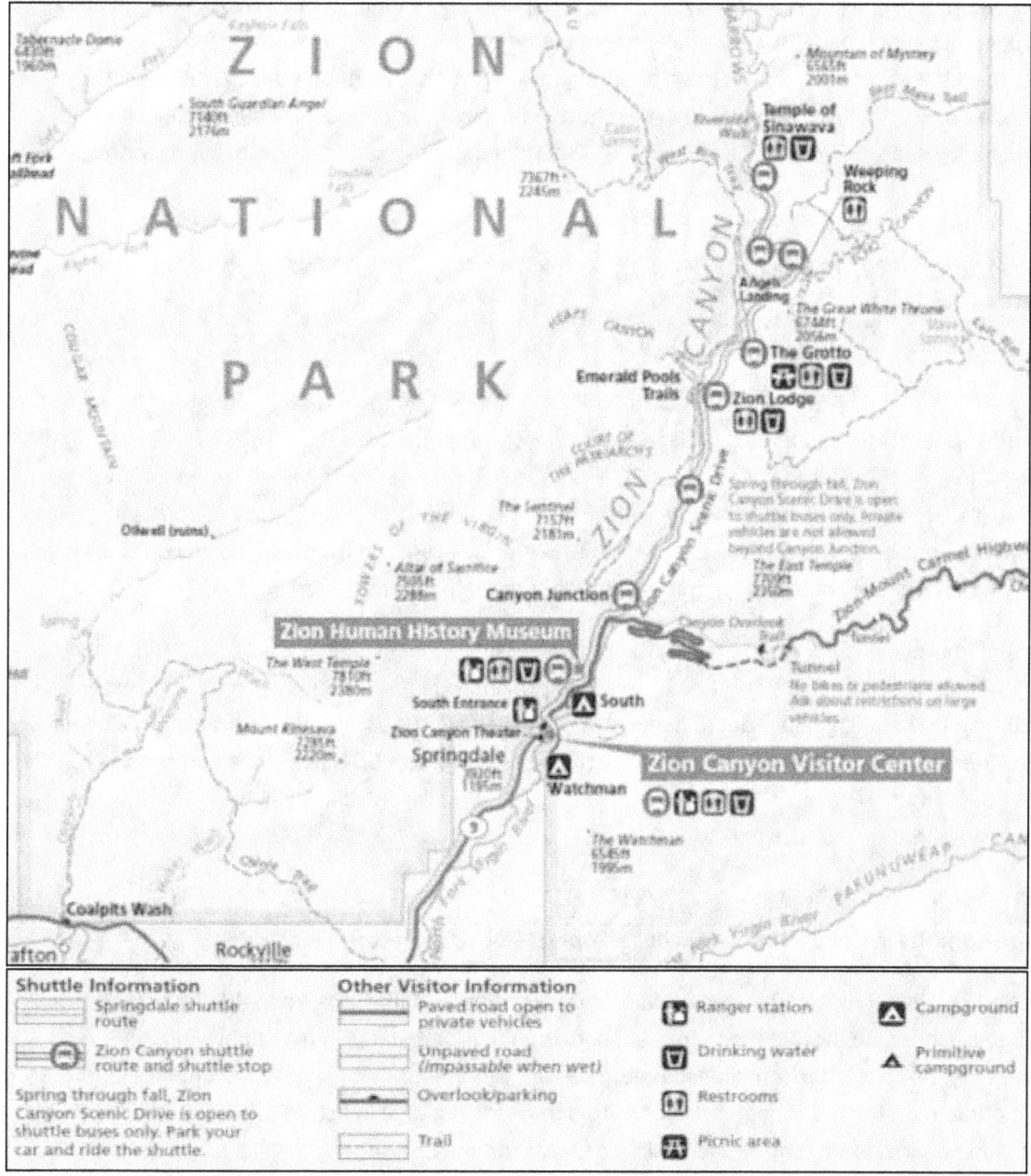

Initial capital investments for the system totaled $12 million. In addition to the shuttle system costs, several million dollars worth of street, landscaping, and sidewalk improvements around shuttle stops in Springdale area around shuttle stops were financed by federal enhancement funds secured by the Utah Department of Transportation. Currently, the operations and maintenance of the system is funded from a transportation fee collected from all visitors as part of the park's entrance fee. In 2009, the park purchased nine new shuttle buses with Federal Lands Highway Program (FLHP), Park Roads and

Parkways Program (PRP) Category III funds and Federal Land Recreational Enhancement Act funds.[50] In the same year, operating costs of the system were roughly $2.7 million, with a total patronage of 3.4 million people, over 80 percent of which were people riding the service within the park. The remainder of riders used the shuttle within the town of Springdale. Additionally, though the overall percentage of handicapped users of the system was low, the shuttle did accommodate over 4,000 wheelchair riders during the 2009 season. Table 23 illustrates the 2009 ridership characteristics of the Zion shuttle.

Table 23 - 2009 Zion shuttle trips. Source: Zion National Park

Year	Total trips	Trips/hour	Wheel chair lift uses	Town trips	Town trips/hour	Park trips	Park trips/hour
2009	3,405,869	74.14	4,263	526,113	56.44	2,870,337	79.81

The shuttle system is now in its 11th season, operating through the concessionaire, Parks Transportation, Inc. The company operates 30 National Park Service (NPS)-owned propane-powered shuttle buses. Roughly 20 of the buses operate within the park and have a capacity of 66 passengers each, and are equipped with trailers. Each full shuttle is calculated to potentially replace up to 25 cars on park roadways. Zion also has two electric trams that hold up to 36 passengers.

The system improves visitor experience at the park by easing access to the main canyon and reducing vehicle noise, emissions, and congestion. In 2000, approximately 75 percent, or 1.5 million passengers used the system, resulting in a reduction of about 1,200 vehicle trips per day and almost 11,000 vehicle miles traveled per day.[51] According to the NPS, the system replaces 50,385 private automobile vehicle miles per day, annually reduces 10,580,866 vehicle miles, and prevents 5,082,254 pounds of CO_2 annually from emitting into the park and surrounding areas.[52]

Acadia National Park, Maine (NPS)

ATS Type – Shuttle system - NPS owned buses, operated by contractor

Acadia National Park (Acadia), located on Mount Desert Island, Maine, preserves 40,000 acres of Atlantic coast shoreline. Acadia is one of the most visited national parks in the country. In 2009, visitation at Acadia exceeded 2 million people. The park is home to many plants and animals, and the tallest mountain on the U.S. Atlantic coast. Visitors to Acadia engage in activities such as hiking, biking, birding, tide pooling, fishing, horseback riding, or scenic driving.[53]

The popularity of Acadia during peak season between May and September, and especially during the months of July and August, leads to congestion and crowded conditions. The park faces the challenges of balancing the area tourism industry with protecting park resources and visitor experiences. In 1999,

---

[50] Telephone conversations with the park.
[51] U.S. Department of Transportation, Federal Highway Administration, Office of Operations. Zion National Park, Accessed July 8, 2010. < http://www.ops.fhwa.dot.gov/publications/mitig_traf_cong/zion_park_case.htm>
[52] Zion National Park Service, Accessed July 13, 2010. http://www.nps.gov/zion/naturescience/green-transit-the-zion-shuttle.htm
[53] National Park System, Acadia. Accessed July 14, 2010. http://www.nps.gov/acad/index.htm

to minimize the negative effects of private automobiles on visitor experience and the environment, the park and its partners implemented the Island Explorer shuttle system.

The Island Explorer is a free, seasonal public transit system that serves Acadia and the surrounding communities. The system operates June 23rd through Columbus Day and connects the park with area campgrounds, motels, the County airport, municipal harbors, and business districts. The system is a public-private partnership involving 20 partners including federal, state, and local agencies that signed an agreement related to the provision of the service. Key partners include Acadia National Park, Maine DOT, Federal Highway Administration, Federal Transit Administration, Downeast Transportation, Inc., Friends of Acadia, and L.L. Bean.

The system has 29 propane-fueled buses that operate on eight routes. The buses are equipped with front and rear bicycle racks, are fully accessible, and are equipped with state of the art technology, including automatic vehicle location, passenger counters, on-board announcements, and real time stop departure signs at select stops. The system is operated by Downeast Transportation Inc. through a contract with Maine DOT and a cooperative agreement with the NPS. There is a staff of 80 employees and as of 2008, an annual operating budget of over $1,000,000.[54]

In 2009, the Island Explorer system carried a total of 367,595 riders. The summer average was 4,238 per day, with a one-day peak of 6,639 riders. The fall average was 1,818, with a one-day peak of 3,703. Continued visitor use of the shuttle system reduces roadway congestion, noise levels, and vehicle emissions. Since 1999, the Island Explorer has provided 3.3 million rides.[55]

The success of the Island Explorer is due to its partnerships and system design. There has been strong cooperation among the NPS, the state of Maine, local communities, and businesses. Visitors and residents ride for free in part as a result of the contribution of funding to the system by local businesses and municipalities. Therefore, even when parking areas in the local area are full, the transit system allows for additional people to access area business districts. Additionally, the system was planned to ensure that adequate parking was provided at campgrounds and motels so that visitors could leave their cars parked at these locations and use the shuttle system to access the downtown and sites in the park.[56] Figure 44 illustrates a typical vehicle in the Island Explorer fleet. Figure 45 illustrates the Island Explorer system map.

---

[54] National Transit Institute. Transit ITS Regional Workshop. December 2008.
[55] Tom Crikelair Associates. Acadia National Park, Island Explorer. Draft Report 7/23/10
[56] National Park Service. Accomplishments in Alternative Transportation. (2003) Pgs. 10 and 13.

Figure 44 - Island Explorer shuttle bus. Source: National Park Service

Figure 45 - Island Explorer shuttle bus system map. Source: Island Explorer, National Park Service

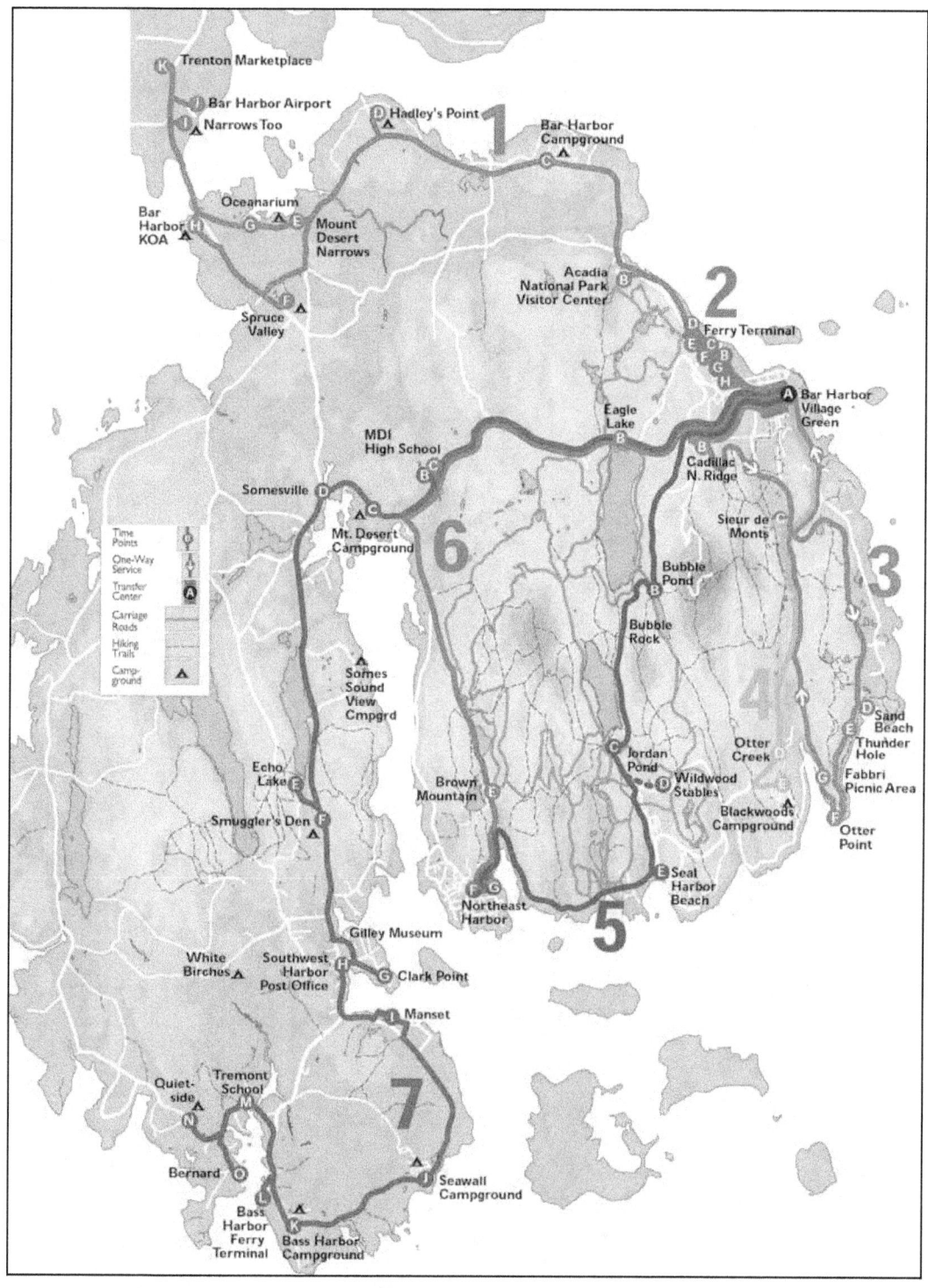

Appendix B – Stakeholder outreach

The following appendix provides the interview guides, summary of key discussion items, and combined stakeholder participant list for the outreach activities conducted as part of the WMNF Alternative Transportation study, which includes:

- Stakeholder engagement workshops – July and August 2010
- Key informant discussions – September 2010
- Alternative Transportation Stakeholder Workshop – December 2010

Stakeholder engagement workshops – July and August, 2010

Each of the engagement workshops had time for three or four questions. While the discussion questions themselves were scripted, conversations between the participants and the moderator were free flowing and covered a range of relevant topics. The questions for the engagement workshops were approximately as follows:

- Say a little bit about how you and your clients access and/or travel through the forest, and how you get around.
  - What are your expectations for access to the WMNF?
  - Have you experienced any issues or inconveniences accessing or traveling through WMNF?
  - Are your experiences on the Kancamagus highway different than in other parts of the forest?
  - Have your expectations been met?
  - Who do you feel is responsible for meeting your expectations in terms of transportation?
- What do you think could be done to improve how people get around in the WMNF? Why?
  - Who shoulders the responsibility for making changes?
  - Who should pay for changes?
- Would you be willing to change your use of and access to the WMNF as part of larger efforts to reduce carbon emissions in the region? By "changing your use of and access to" I'm referring to options such as shuttle services, carpooling, disincentives, or being flexible in terms of when you access the forest.
- What are your thoughts about coordinated transportation? Should people be working together to change transportation offerings throughout the WMNF? What would that coordination look like?
  - Would you be interested in coordinating with other users/providers?
  - What are some opportunities for coordination among users/providers that you see?
  - What issues need to be resolved regarding coordinated transportation?

Table 24 - Engagement workshop participants and affiliations.

Organization	Name
Waterville Valley Transit Authority	Mark Decoteau
PSU Outdoor Center	Rodney Ekstrom
Institute for New Hampshire Studies	Mark Okrant
Division of Travel and Tourism Development	Lori Harnois
New Hampshire Branding Initiative	Samantha Kenney Maltais
White Mountain Attractions	Jayne O'Connor
North Country Health Consortium	Martha McLeod
Friends of Pondicherry	Dave Govatski
Mt Washington Auto Road	Howie Wemyss
Plymouth Transport Central	Patsy Kendall
North Country Transit	Beverly Raymond
White Mountain Transit Authority	Michael Curreri
Waterville Valley Cab Company	Joe Corrigan
Plymouth Transport Central	Patsy Kendall
North Country Transit	Beverly Raymond
White Mountain Transit Authority	Michael Curreri
Waterville Valley Cab Company	Joe Corrigan

Key informant discussions – September 2010

General questions (for all interviewees):

In terms of the local area (communities surrounding the WMNF)

- What are the biggest transportation strengths?
- Weaknesses?
- Opportunities?
- Threats?
- What are the challenges and opportunities for implementing or promoting alternative means of travel e.g. biking, walking, and taking transit to locations near or in the WMNF?
- What current or planned projects in the area that may directly affect WMNF and alternative transportation planning?
- What opportunities to do you see for transit service in the area to facilitate travel to popular destinations in the WMNF?
- Other comments/ideas regarding the lack of accessibility for non-motorists in the WMNF area?

Questions for NH DOT Bicycle Pedestrian Program

1. What are NHDOT planning criteria for bicycle and pedestrian facilities to be integrated into highway projects or to be developed as independent projects?
2. The North Country Council Regional Transportation Plan (2009) mentions that an objective of NHDOT regarding bicycle and pedestrian activities is a statewide plan for the integration of

recreation trails with other bicycle/pedestrian facilities been developed by NHDOT in cooperation with the NH DRED. What is the status of this objective? What are the implications for utilitarian and recreational bicycle/pedestrian facilities on/through or near WMNF?

    a. Status / update on the Lincoln to Woodstock bike path?

    b. Status / update on the Notch to Notch bike path?

    c. Are there any well-documented conflict points between bicycles, pedestrians, and automobiles on roads in or near WMNF? Anecdotal areas of concern?

    d. Where is NHDOT in terms of the schedule for Transportation Enhancement Program funding allocations?

Questions for North Country Council

1. The White Mountains Corridor Mgmt Plan (2003) speaks to the goals of the WM Byway Council to make the byway loops safer for bicycle travel and that construction or reconstruction allow for adequate shoulder for bike and pedestrian use and that cyclist bypasses be constructed in areas of high congestion to facilitate safer travel.

    a. Have these goals been met in new construction/rehabilitation along the byway?

    b. What are NCC's top transportation needs in communities and roadways near WMNF? Alternative transportation needs?

    c. Are there any well-documented conflict points between bicycles, pedestrians, and automobiles on roads in or near WMNF? Anecdotal areas of concern?

    d. Is the draft TIP 2011-2020- June 2, 2010? When is the final TIP being decided?

    e. How does NCC support communities or the WMNF in seeking Transportation Enhancement Program funding?

Questions for White Mountain Attractions

1. Describe the membership structure and benefits of being a part of the White Mountains Attractions group.

2. Can you speak to the working relationship between WMA and WMNF? Is WMA open to collaborative marketing opportunities?

3. Much of the traveler information on the WMA site is car-centric. Are there opportunities to provide more information about existing public transportation options on the WMA website?

Questions for North Country Transit

1. Please describe the following characteristics of the North Country Transit system

    a. Rough # of vehicles / types of vehicles (e.g. coaches, shuttles, etc.)

    b. What are the primary trip origins?

    c. What are the primary trip destinations?

    d. What are times of peak demand?

    e. Seasonal

    f. Weekday / weekend

    g. Daily

    h. How is your system marketed?

    i. How do customers learn about your service?

2. How do you coordinate with other systems – public or private (e.g. transfer time and locations, route coordination, shared dispatch center, collocated facilities and maintenance, vehicle sharing, etc.)
3. Why or how would adapting your system for recreational use be challenging? (Examples in terms of infrastructure, policy, operations etc.)
4. Do you see opportunities for coordination with (e.g. in terms of service and marketing) with:
    a. Other transit systems?
    b. WMNF? Shopping centers / hotels / restaurants?
    c. Regarding the new Conway flex-route service connector from W. Ossipee to Conway and N.Conway, are there opportunities to consider this route as a means to facilitate weekend travelers to WMNF?
    d. Are there opportunities for creating a transportation center, potentially similar to the Concord Transportation Center in Lincoln, Conway/North Conway, or Littleton, Gorham, and Plymouth (or Campton)?
5. Are there opportunities to create park and ride lots that serve the WMNF area, that could potentially connect with existing shuttle services (e.g. AMC), or future services?

Questions for Concord Coach Lines /C&J Bus Co.
1. Are there opportunities to coordinate with other public (e.g. AMC shuttles) or private transit systems in the WMNF area?
2. What is the process for expanding a scheduled bus service?
3. What are the best opportunities you see for expanding service to provide for more regional connections to/from the WM area?
4. Bicycles are accepted on board when space is available. If travelers with bicycles become more common, would there be opportunities to reserve or pay for space to carry bicycles as a means to ensure their accommodation?
5. In your opinion, where would a transportation center (similar to the Concord Transportation Center) be most needed?

Questions for NH DRED
1. What are the transportation planning/implementation priorities for DRED?
2. How does DRED approach transportation planning and needs in the region and in particular the WMNF area?
3. How does DRED work/coordinate with WMNF activities/initiatives, planning, needs etc.?
4. Is the concept of car-free travel to and through the WMNF area viable?
5. What transportation infrastructure [e.g. parking lots, maintenance areas, fueling stations, etc. (assumed for state park vehicle fleets)] does DRED own/maintain/manage? Are there opportunities for shared use of any of these facilities? For example, the use of parking lots as potential shuttle stop locations? The shared use of maintenance / storage / fueling areas?

Table 25 - Key informant discussion participants and affiliations.

Organization	Name
NH DOT Bicycle/Ped program	Larry Keniston
NH DOT Bicycle/Ped program	Jerry Moore
Transportation Planner	Mary Deppe
White Mountain Attractions	Jayne O'Connor
Retired USFS / Friends of Pondicherry	Dave Govatsky
NH Division of Parks and Recreation	Ted Austin
Tri-County Communtiy Action Program	Beverly Raymond
C&J Bus Company	Jim Jalbert
Concord Coach Lines	Ken Hunter

Alternative Transportation Stakeholder Workshop – December 2010

Exercise A: Full group discussion on transportation issues

Objective: To solicit feedback from the stakeholder group on the individual transportation "issues" identified by category as part of this study.

Process:

- Discussion will be held with the entire group (theatre style)
- Each issue area (bicycle, pedestrian, wayfinding, etc.) will be discussed separately.
- Each participant will have a full list of categorized issue areas on an 8.5 by 11 paper.
- Issue area categories will be displayed on individual PPT slides.
- Flip chart note taking will include:
- General comments
- Addition of issues to any of the category areas/or addition of new categories

Focus of discussion will center around two main questions:

- Do you agree with that the transportation issues identified are appropriate/correct to the current conditions you experience while traveling in and around the WMNF? *(For example, in your experience, is a lack of signage or poor signage an issue that you experience in your area travels?)*
- Are there specific transportation issues that are not identified that should be?

Key points:

- Issues were gathered from various previous studies, and key stakeholder discussions, field observations, and analysis completed as part of this study.
- Issues identified are generally specific to transportation, safety, mobility, and access to sites and areas in and around WMNF.

- The information from this exercise will be used to inform the next exercise, and ultimately the final report and recommended next steps for the Forest Service and its partners.

Exercise B: Breakout small group discussion on transportation options

Objective: To solicit feedback from the stakeholder group on the individual transportation "options" identified by category as part of this study.

Process:

- Break stakeholders into 4 small groups (of rough equal size) for each of the 4 category areas: bicycle, pedestrian, wayfinding, policy/planning.
- Each group will have 10 minutes to discuss:
  - Identified options
  - Add options not on the list
  - Come to consensus as a group on the top two options they would like to see implemented/worked towards
- A "host" is stationed at each category area. The job of the host is to:
  - Explain directions to the group
  - Keep them on track/watch the time
  - Take notes
    - Additions to options are written on the printed options poster
    - Key points and notes will be written on a templates
  - Report results from each group at the end of the rounds of conversation
- There are four rounds of conversation with everyone, except the host, moving to a new category area for each round.
- After the four rounds of small-group conversations, the full group reconvenes for "group synthesis."
- Each category group will report back to the larger group on any additions to the list (explaining those additions) and the options that received the top votes for each round (1-4)

Table 26 - Alternative Transportation Stakeholder Workshop participants and affiliations.

Organization	Name
WMNF	Ken Allen
AMC	Susan Arnold
WMNF	Bill Dauer
North Country Council	Mary Deppe
NH DOT	Dean Eastman
Friends of Pondicherry	David Govatski
NH DOT	Larry Keniston
Northern Community Investment Corporation	Samantha Kenney Maltais
WMNF	Stacy Lemieux
WMNF	Susan Mathieu
North Country Health Consortium	Martha McLeod
NH DOT	Jerry Moore
North Country Transit - Tri County CAP	Bev Raymond
AMC	Chris Thayer

www.ingramcontent.com/pod-product-compliance
Lightning Source LLC
Chambersburg PA
CBHW081105290526
45795CB00006B/2001